Dangerous Times Book Series

Dangerous Times: The Americas Under the Shadows of Terror

© 2025 Johan Obdola

All rights reserved. Revised Version

ISBN: 978-1-77524-538-4

No part of this publication may be reproduced, stored in a retrieval system, or transmitted in any form or by any means — electronic, mechanical, photocopying, recording, or otherwise — without prior written permission of the author, except in the case of brief quotations used in critical articles or reviews.

This book is a work of non-fiction. Names, characters, businesses, places, events, and incidents are either the product of the author's professional experience and research, or are used in a factual context. Any resemblance to actual persons, living or dead, or actual events is coincidental unless otherwise stated.

Distributed worldwide via IngramSpark

First printing: 2025

Canada I U.S. I International

"With deep respect and heartfelt gratitude,
this book is dedicated to the extraordinary women and men
who have made the ultimate sacrifice,
as well as to those currently serving in police, military, and security forces around the world.

They are the unsung guardians —
whose unwavering resolve defends our societies
from the persistent shadows of violence, corruption, and terror.

In an era marked by systemic collapse and relentless hybrid threats,
they remain the frontline of resistance,
upholding peace, law, and dignity where many have looked away.

To you who pick up this book,
thank you for giving my words a chance.

And to life —
my greatest teacher —
a journey etched in pain,
but also illuminated by laughter, memory,
and an unbroken love for a brighter tomorrow."

-Johan Obdola

Acknowledgements

I would like to express my deepest gratitude to the global members and senior advisors of IOSI Global, the international platform I founded with the mission to confront organized crime, terrorism, and transnational threats with truth, courage, and strategic clarity.

Your commitment to security, human dignity, and international cooperation continues to inspire my work.

Together, we face the shadows of this world — not with fear, but with ethical resolve.

To the brave women and men in law enforcement, military, and intelligence services across the Americas and beyond — this book is a testament to your daily, often unseen struggle to protect what remains of order, sovereignty, and hope.

To the leaders and guardians of Indigenous Nations in Canada, especially Roxanne Lindley, Sherry Lindley, and my dear friend Wayne Shalil — thank you for granting me a place of peace in the heart of the wild, where the land itself spoke healing and truth. Your generosity and spirit shaped key passages of this book.

And finally, to every citizen who dares to care — who resists silence, questions power, and believes that justice must prevail — I thank you for walking this path with me.

This book was born from scars, silence, and struggle.

But it lives now as a voice of resistance — and a call to remembrance.

Author's Note

Dear Reader,

As we embark on this journey through the pages of DANGEROUS TIMES, I write to you with a profound sense of urgency and purpose. This book is not just a recounting of threats — it is a declaration of resistance, a testimony of lived struggle, and a reflection of our shared responsibility to confront the forces that endanger liberty, security, and truth in our time.

The first volume of this series, **DANGEROUS TIMES: The Americas Under the Shadows of Terror,** is more than a chronicle of events. It is born from the frontlines — from my own trajectory as a counter-narcotics officer in Venezuela, a homeland I was forced to leave after facing corruption, death threats, and exile. It draws from my later work as an intelligence strategist navigating the darkest corridors of global crime, ideological extremism, and institutional collapse.

Each chapter you will read is grounded in real-world encounters — from the silence of political betrayal to the adrenaline of covert operations; from the brutal truths of narco-governance to the moral fractures within institutions once meant to protect us. These pages trace the sinister evolution of Venezuela from a wounded republic into a systemic narco-terrorist state — not in abstraction, but in visceral, human terms.

This revised edition, released in August 2025, comes at a pivotal moment in history: following the official designation of the Cartel de los Soles as a Foreign Terrorist Organization by the United States, and shortly after the Tren de Aragua was also listed as a global transnational criminal threat. These events confirm what many of us have denounced for over two decades — that the Venezuelan regime has ceased to be a government, and has become a hybrid criminal enterprise, using the mask of sovereignty to export terror, launder billions, and systematically dismantle the democratic and legal fabric of the Western Hemisphere.

The pace of this transformation has accelerated dramatically. What once seemed confined to Venezuela now spreads like a malignant force — into Colombia, Ecuador, Chile, Mexico, the Caribbean, Europe, and even the Middle East through strategic alliances with Iran, Hezbollah, Russia, and Turkey. And yet, despite mounting evidence, many nations remain paralyzed — complicit through silence or constrained by their economic dependencies and geopolitical calculations.

This book is not written for those who wish to look away. It is written for those who understand that when a state becomes the crime itself, its collapse becomes a global concern. It is written for those who still believe in the power of truth — however uncomfortable — and in the necessity of action, however costly.

And yet, this is not a story of defeat. It is, above all, a testament to human resilience. Wherever criminal power rises, there are still women and men — known and unknown — who rise against it with courage, ethics, and vision. I dedicate this work to them. To those who resist not with hatred, but with purpose.

Let these pages be more than a record. Let them be a warning, a tool, and a beacon. May they ignite in you the conviction that security, justice, and dignity are not given — they are earned, defended, and reclaimed.

Thank you for walking with me through these Dangerous Times.

With unwavering resolve,

Johan Obdola

Prologue

*T*he world today appears to be descending into a deliberate disorder — a collapse not born of chaos alone, but of design. From where I stand, we are not merely confronting a pandemic and its evolving strains. We are facing far more insidious viruses — corruption, radicalization, and systemic criminality — all of them man-made, all of them accelerating.

What began as isolated crises has coalesced into a dark global architecture: a nexus of organized crime, ideological extremism, human trafficking, narco-terrorism, and modern slavery — operating across borders, exploiting institutional weakness, and redefining the rules of power.

The familiar world order is disoriented. And we, as citizens, security professionals, and leaders, are struggling to keep pace with its engineered unraveling.

So we must ask:

Is there a deeper story unfolding?
Are terrorist networks and criminal syndicates working hand in hand with populist regimes, rogue states, and corrupted political elites — to reshape the very DNA of modern society?
Is this the product of a hidden strategy, or are we witnessing a systemic metamorphosis of civilization under pressure?

I do not ask these questions rhetorically.
I have seen the answers firsthand.
And I have lived their consequences.

"I have witnessed these dynamics in my journey and have been fighting against them.

My homeland has been meticulously manipulated into becoming the inaugural Narco-Terrorist State in the annals of the Americas.

Under one sinister umbrella, corrupt officials, criminals, drug traffickers, genocidal acts, and terrorists have come together to govern Venezuela.

Despite this imminent threat, the world seems to falter in its ability to adequately address the issue.

This is just one example of many."

This book begins with that reality.
But it does not end in despair.
It is a call to remember, to resist, and to rebuild.
-Johan Obdola

Dangerous Times: The Americas Under the Shadows of Terror is a revelatory chronicle of the rise of terrorism, narco-terrorism, and transnational crime — and how their convergence is rapidly redefining security and sovereignty throughout the hemisphere.

Each chapter begins with a sharp, symbolic reflection — a prelude to the unfolding crisis. The opening chapters recount my personal pursuit of justice: a direct confrontation with the forces that hollowed out Venezuela, and now threaten global democratic resilience.

This book is not fiction. It is drawn from lived operations, real victims, and the scars of war. I have lost colleagues, friends, and partners in the field. Many fell to drug cartels shielded by political and military protection. And many more remain in silence — trapped in systems of fear, censorship, and impunity.

I write this not only as a former intelligence officer, but as a human being who has seen his country transformed into the prototype of a criminal state. Under the false banner of revolution, Venezuela has been looted of its wealth — its gold, oil, gas, and strategic minerals — by a criminal elite allied with terrorist groups, cartels, and geopolitical opportunists.

But the story does not end at Venezuela's borders. This book expands to expose how this criminal matrix now stretches across Latin America, into the United States, Canada, Africa, the Middle East, Asia, and Europe — forming a transcontinental web of corruption, insurgency, and influence.

We face a global surge in radicalization, terrorism, organized crime, and narco-terrorism. Their enclaves grow inside our democracies, exploiting migration, weaponizing information, and poisoning institutions.

Dangerous Times maps this transformation. It examines how regimes use economic warfare, asymmetric violence, and geopolitical proxies to weaken the Western Hemisphere from within. It investigates how groups like Hezbollah, FARC, ELN, ISIS, and Al Qaeda operate alongside narco-networks — creating a hemispheric threat system unlike anything we've seen before.

This book also lifts the veil on money laundering at scale — implicating politicians, banks, public entities, and private corporations in a vast scheme of illicit finance that sustains terrorism and criminal expansion. It is a testimony to how corruption is no longer a local affliction, but a global operating system.

And yet, this is not just a book of warning — it is a call to resist, a commitment to expose what must no longer remain hidden. Through the Dangerous Times series, we will engage with some of the world's leading voices in security, intelligence, and resistance.

This book is for those who refuse to be silent.

It is for those who understand that survival is not enough — we must act.

This is a time for clarity, courage, and strategy.

Welcome to Dangerous Times.

Let us begin.

Definition

Terror:

The term terror is commonly defined as an overwhelming and paralyzing sense of fear. But in the context of modern power structures, terror transcends emotional response — it becomes an instrument of control.

In political, military, and psychological domains, terror is often strategically manufactured and weaponized. It is not merely a consequence of violence, but a calculated method of influence — deployed by governments, armed groups, criminal networks, and ideological movements to destabilize, silence, and subjugate.

Whether imposed through bombings, beheadings, digital threats, political purges, or televised brutality, the objective remains the same: to fracture human resilience, manipulate perception, and reshape behavior. When fear becomes currency, terror becomes policy.

In this framework, terror is not an isolated act — it is part of a systemic architecture of coercion. It blurs the line between defender and aggressor, between security and authoritarianism. Under the banner of protection, entire societies are conditioned to accept surveillance, censorship, militarization, and moral compromise — all in the name of safety.

The ultimate danger of terror lies not just in its violence, but in its normalization. When fear becomes routine, and terror becomes ambient, oppression no longer needs justification — it becomes embedded in law, media, and culture.

Terror, then, is not simply a tactic of the enemy.

It is a tool that may be used — and misused — by anyone who fears truth more than conflict.

Terrorism:

Terrorism is one of the most politically charged and strategically manipulated terms in modern security discourse. At its core, it refers to the calculated use of violence or the threat thereof — often targeting civilians — to instill fear and advance political, ideological, or religious objectives.

But beyond this operational definition lies a far more contested battlefield.

While traditionally associated with non-state actors — insurgents, extremists, guerrillas — the evolving reality of the 21st century demands a broader lens. Today, states themselves engage in terrorism, either directly or through proxies, using asymmetric tactics, covert operations, and psychological warfare to enforce compliance, suppress dissent, and project fear.

The motivations behind terrorism are not static. They range from ideological fanaticism and separatist identity movements to geopolitical sabotage, narco-terror financing, and authoritarian consolidation. Terrorism is both a tool of the weak — seeking attention or disruption — and a weapon of the powerful — used to fracture populations, delegitimize opposition, or wage proxy wars.

The most dangerous dimension of terrorism is its interpretive fluidity. What is branded as terrorism in one nation is celebrated as resistance in another. Definitions shift based on political agendas, cultural narratives, and intelligence framing. Entire populations have been demonized as "terrorists," while certain regimes with clear patterns of state-sponsored terror remain immune from international accountability.

In this sense, terrorism is not only a tactic.

It is a label — weaponized through language, deployed selectively, and deeply embedded in the machinery of modern propaganda.

Understanding terrorism, therefore, requires more than a security perspective. It demands ethical clarity, geopolitical literacy, and the courage to confront uncomfortable truths — including the complicity of global powers in sustaining the very violence they publicly condemn.

Narco-terrorism / Narcoterrorism:

Narco-terrorism describes the strategic convergence between the global narcotics trade and acts of terrorism, creating a hybrid threat architecture that fuses criminality, violence, ideological warfare, and political destabilization.

At its core, narco-terrorism refers to the use of drug trafficking to fund terrorist operations — a phenomenon where militant groups rely on narcotics production, transit, and sales to finance their agendas, acquire arms, recruit combatants, and expand territorial control. But the term has evolved far beyond its original scope.

Coined in 1983 by Peruvian President Fernando Belaúnde Terry to describe cartel-style attacks on anti-narcotics police, narco-terrorism has since expanded into a transnational model — where drug syndicates adopt terror tactics to control populations and intimidate governments, and terrorist groups embrace drug trafficking as a sustainable revenue stream.

What emerges is a fluid, adaptable ecosystem in which criminal and political actors form symbiotic alliances, merging ideological rhetoric with the ruthless logic of profit. Cartels use terror to enforce territorial dominance. Insurgents use drug revenues to buy geopolitical relevance.

In this system:
- Drug routes become corridors of armed insurgency.
- Political regimes collude with cartels to consolidate authoritarian power.

- Corruption becomes systemic — not incidental, but structural and intentional.

The line between ideological terrorism and organized crime dissolves.

The result: a new form of criminal sovereignty — one that operates through intimidation, manipulation, and state capture.

Today, narco-terrorism is not limited to remote jungles or failed states.

Its reach extends into parliaments, judicial systems, ports, banks, and international diplomacy. And nowhere is this more evident than in Venezuela — the world's first fully operational narco-terrorist state, where the fusion of cartel economics, ideological authoritarianism, and international terrorism has become a model exported across Latin America and beyond.

Addressing narco-terrorism requires more than traditional counterterrorism or anti-drug efforts. It demands:
- Integrated intelligence operations
- Uncompromising international cooperation
- Strategic disruption of financial ecosystems
- And above all, political will to expose and dismantle the networks that enable it

Narco-terrorism is not just a threat.

It is a system of power — globalized, weaponized, and increasingly normalized.

Radicalization:

Radicalization encompasses the intricate process through which individuals or groups undergo a transformative journey, embracing radical, extremist, or fringe beliefs, ideologies, or viewpoints. This evolution typically involves a departure from moderate or conventional beliefs towards more extreme positions, manifesting in radicalized attitudes, behaviours, and actions.

At its core, radicalization represents a complex interplay of social, political, economic, and psychological factors that contribute to the adoption of extremist ideologies. These factors may include feelings of marginalization, perceived injustices, ideological indoctrination, social alienation, and exposure to radicalizing influences, such as propaganda, charismatic leaders, or online extremist communities.

The radicalization process is dynamic and nonlinear, varying in intensity, duration, and outcome for each individual or group. It may unfold gradually over time or be triggered by specific events or experiences, leading individuals to embrace radical ideologies and, in some cases, resort to acts of violence or terrorism to advance their extremist agendas.

Understanding the mechanisms and drivers of radicalization is crucial for developing effective prevention, intervention, and counter-radicalization strategies. By addressing root causes, promoting social cohesion, fostering critical thinking skills, and providing alternative narratives, societies can mitigate the risks associated with radicalization and prevent the spread of extremist ideologies.

Transnational Crime:

When discussing transnational crime, we are delving into the realm of criminal activities that transcend national boundaries, orchestrated by sophisticated and organized criminal syndicates. This nefarious spectrum of criminal endeavours encompasses a wide array of illicit activities that traverse multiple jurisdictions, facilitated by the interconnectedness of the globalized world.

Examples of transnational crime include but are not limited to:

Drug Trafficking: The illegal production, distribution, and sale of narcotics across international borders, fueling addiction, violence, and corruption worldwide.

Human Trafficking: The coerced recruitment, transportation, and exploitation of individuals across borders for purposes such as forced labour, sexual exploitation, or organ trafficking.

Cybercrime: Criminal activities perpetrated through digital networks, including hacking, identity theft, online fraud, and cyber espionage, with perpetrators operating from various locations around the globe.

Money Laundering: The process of disguising the origins of illegally obtained funds to make them appear legitimate, often involving the movement of illicit proceeds across multiple jurisdictions through complex financial transactions.

Arms Trafficking:

The illicit trade and cross-border movement of firearms, ammunition, explosives, and military-grade weaponry constitutes a core pillar of transnational crime. This dark market fuels armed conflicts, sustains terrorist organizations, empowers violent non-state actors, and undermines state sovereignty. Arms trafficking thrives in regions of weak governance and porous borders, often facilitated by corrupt intermediaries and rogue regimes.

Environmental Crime:

Frequently overlooked but deeply corrosive, environmental crime involves the illegal exploitation of natural resources—such as wildlife poaching, illicit logging, illegal mining, and unregulated fishing. These acts not only devastate ecosystems and contribute to climate degradation but also fund criminal networks that profit from the plunder of the planet's biodiversity. Environmental crime is increasingly recognized as a strategic vector of transnational crime due to its links with corruption, trafficking, and state fragility.

Corruption, Governance, and Security: Unraveling the Intricate Web.

In the vast and shifting landscape of global insecurity, one force remains the silent architect behind the collapse of democratic institutions, the rise of criminal empires, and the deepening erosion of public trust: corruption.

While terrorism, narco-terrorism, radicalization, and transnational crime are often analyzed as distinct phenomena, they are in fact interdependent mechanisms, tightly woven together by a common enabler—corruption. It is this pervasive and systemic corrosion of integrity within institutions that fuels a multidimensional crisis, where impunity reigns and lawlessness becomes normalized.

At the core of this global affliction lies the decomposition of governance. Corrupt political elites, military officials, police commanders, judges, and bureaucrats create a shadow ecosystem where loyalty is traded for silence, and public duty is replaced by self-interest. In such environments, criminal syndicates are not just tolerated—they are empowered. Borders blur, sovereign institutions are infiltrated, and the instruments of state authority are weaponized to serve illicit networks.

Corruption is the oxygen of transnational crime. It enables the cross-border trafficking of narcotics, arms, humans, and illicit capital. It cloaks terrorist operatives in layers of bureaucratic protection. And it transforms security forces—from protectors of the people into guardians of criminal enterprises. The result is a distortion of the state itself—a mutation where governance is no longer in service of the citizen, but in submission to illicit power.

But the reach of corruption extends beyond security—it penetrates the social fabric. In communities where corruption dominates, radicalization finds fertile ground. Disillusioned youth, betrayed by the failure of basic services and justice systems, turn to violent ideologies and criminal identity structures. Injustice becomes their daily reality. Extremism becomes their language of resistance.

Worse still, narco-terrorist regimes—like the one now entrenched in Venezuela—demonstrate how corruption can be elevated into an operational model of governance. These regimes are not failed states. They are criminal states—intentionally constructed architectures of impunity, where political authority, criminality, and ideological extremism coexist as a singular force.

The implications for global security are stark. Without confronting corruption, no counterterrorism strategy will succeed. Without dismantling corrupt patronage networks, no war on drugs can be won. Without restoring the integrity of governance, no society will achieve lasting peace.

To effectively disrupt this web of interlinked threats, we must:
- Establish independent, incorruptible institutions that operate above partisan or criminal influence.

- Implement transparent systems of oversight and accountability across all branches of government.
- Strengthen judicial independence and protect investigative journalism and whistleblowers.
- Promote civic education and critical thinking, especially among youth vulnerable to ideological manipulation.
- Foster transnational cooperation, intelligence sharing, and rapid response mechanisms to combat illicit financial flows and cross-border criminal networks.

This is not merely a security agenda—it is a battle for moral sovereignty, a call to reclaim the very notion of the public good. The time to act is not tomorrow. It is now.

Funding and Financing: Unveiling the Corrupt Underbelly:

Terrorism and narco-terrorism are not sustained by ideology alone—they are empowered by money, logistics, and betrayal from within. At the heart of their longevity lies an uncomfortable and devastating truth: they are funded, protected, and often enabled by the very institutions meant to oppose them.

The financial undercurrents that sustain terrorist networks and narco-criminal enterprises run deep through political institutions, law enforcement agencies, and transnational financial systems. Corruption is not merely a vulnerability—it is a strategic asset for these organizations, a lifeline that turns public servants into accomplices and national institutions into weapons of impunity.

From municipal police chiefs to high-ranking military officials, from customs officers to cabinet ministers, individuals have been co-opted, bribed, and in many cases willfully recruited into the machinery of illicit power. These actors serve as the facilitators of crime—whether through silence, protection, or active participation.

Tactics of infiltration and co-optation include:
- Bribery and kickbacks, ensuring that drug shipments pass unchecked and terrorist operatives remain invisible.

• Embezzlement and diversion of public funds, rechanneling state resources into criminal hands.

• Manipulation of procurement contracts, allowing criminal-linked companies to launder money or gain access to strategic assets.

• Direct collusion with cartels or terrorist networks, offering intelligence, passports, weapons, or transport in exchange for personal gain.

This corrupt ecosystem is not passive—it is operational. It sabotages investigations, cripples border enforcement, compromises counter-terrorism operations, and enables the laundering of billions in criminal profits through real estate, offshore accounts, and "legitimate" enterprises.

Even international aid and anti-drug funding can be diverted or weaponized under corrupt regimes, especially those that masquerade as states while functioning as criminal conglomerates. Venezuela, Afghanistan, and parts of Central America offer chilling case studies.

Worse still, the perception of corruption itself weakens state legitimacy, erodes public confidence, and empowers radical and criminal actors to claim moral superiority. When the public sees no justice, they stop believing in the system—and in that vacuum, extremism and crime thrive.

To dismantle this financial architecture of terror, bold and coordinated action is essential:

• Implement global transparency mechanisms to trace and freeze assets linked to terrorist or criminal networks.

• Strengthen oversight of public procurement and financial institutions, including crypto and real estate sectors.

• Enforce international anti-corruption treaties and sanction officials who enable or benefit from illicit networks.

• Build independent anti-corruption units with investigative authority insulated from political influence.

• Train and equip whistleblowers, investigative journalists, and civil society watchdogs, as frontline defenders of integrity.

Ultimately, the war against narco-terrorism and transnational extremism will be won or lost on the battlefield of governance. Where corruption thrives, terrorism is funded. Where transparency reigns, security begins.

State Weakness and Infiltration: Unraveling the Nexus of Terrorism, Radicalization, and Transnational Crime:

In the architecture of global security, the weakness of the state is the breach through which chaos enters. Wherever institutions are fragile, compromised, or corrupted, the foundations of national sovereignty erode—inviting infiltration by the most dangerous forces of our time: terrorism, radicalization, and transnational organized crime.

States plagued by endemic corruption, judicial paralysis, and unaccountable power structures are not simply dysfunctional—they are vulnerable targets and, increasingly, unwilling accomplices. Criminal and extremist actors thrive in these environments, not by overpowering the state, but by penetrating and hijacking its very mechanisms.

The infiltration process is systematic and multi-layered:

- Security agencies are compromised through bribery, political appointments, or ideological co-optation, allowing terrorists or cartel operatives to obtain intelligence, evade capture, and execute attacks with impunity.
- Border and customs controls are neutralized, turning national frontiers into corridors of illicit trafficking—from arms and narcotics to human smuggling and terror logistics.
- Judicial and prosecutorial systems are weaponized or neutralized, ensuring that key figures remain untouchable and that impunity is institutionalized.
- Radical or criminal entities assume influence within ministries, police forces, or even parliaments, positioning themselves as shadow powers beneath—or inside—the legitimate state.

This infiltration is not only operational—it is existential. It undermines public trust, deepens social polarization, and creates the perfect storm for violent radicalization. In communities already marginalized or disenfranchised, the failure of the state becomes the rationale for extremist ideologies to take root. When hope is denied, radical alternatives become seductive.

Moreover, the decay of the state accelerates in a self-perpetuating cycle: corruption breeds impunity, impunity enables crime, and crime reinforces the collapse of governance. In this vacuum, the rule of law gives way to the rule of networks—narco-networks, terror networks, extremist networks.

Strategic Response: From Fragility to Fortification

To disrupt this nexus, states must engage in bold and irreversible reforms, not merely cosmetic gestures. This includes:

• Securing the institutional firewall: Establishing truly independent anti-corruption bodies with prosecutorial authority.

• Professionalizing and depoliticizing security forces, backed by international training and vetting mechanisms.

• Implementing rigorous asset-tracing and anti-money laundering frameworks to uncover the hidden financial pipelines of infiltration.

• Building civic legitimacy by ensuring transparency, justice delivery, and equitable public service at the local level—where the state is often most invisible.

• Strengthening regional and global intelligence cooperation to identify and dismantle transnational infiltration strategies early and decisively.

This is not merely a task of good governance—it is a matter of national survival.

In a world where threats do not knock but breach, where enemies wear suits as easily as uniforms, and where betrayal often comes from within, the strength and integrity of the state is our last line of defense.

Exploitation of Socioeconomic Grievances:

Radicalization does not emerge in a vacuum. It often grows in the shadow of systemic corruption, feeding on deep socioeconomic fractures and the pervasive sense of betrayal by institutions that fail to deliver justice, opportunity, and dignity. In this context, corruption is not just a governance failure—it is an accelerant for extremism.

Corruption perpetuates cycles of poverty, inequality, and disenfranchisement. When people are denied access to healthcare, education, employment, or protection under the law—not because of a lack of national resources, but due to the theft and mismanagement of those resources—the result is a profound moral injury. Marginalized individuals and communities become alienated not only from the state but from the very idea of democratic participation or social contract.

This is where extremist ideologies find fertile soil.

Weaponizing Grievances

Extremist groups are not only ideological machines—they are strategic social operators. They excel at identifying and weaponizing legitimate grievances, reframing systemic injustices caused by corruption as proof of moral decay or illegitimacy of the ruling order. To the disillusioned youth, the unemployed graduate, the rural family abandoned by public services, these groups offer:
- A cause that speaks to their suffering
- A narrative that explains their injustice
- A mission that promises purpose, retribution, and identity

By positioning themselves as the antidote to corruption and moral failure, extremist actors portray their violence not as criminal, but as righteous revolution.

Corruption Undermines State Legitimacy

When corruption becomes endemic, the moral authority of the state collapses. Citizens no longer view institutions as mechanisms of justice or progress—but as instruments of exploitation. In this vacuum of trust, extremist movements often fill the void with promises of moral purity, divine justice, or radical equality.

This erosion of state legitimacy also weakens community resilience. Civil society becomes fragmented, political participation dwindles, and polarization intensifies—all conditions that enable radical actors to penetrate and recruit with minimal resistance.

Strategic Countermeasures

To neutralize the link between corruption and radicalization, states must move beyond security-centric responses and address the root causes of grievance and abandonment:

- Anti-corruption must be national security policy: Transparency, independent oversight, and public accountability must be elevated as strategic imperatives.
- Empowerment must replace marginalization: Governments must invest in inclusive development, equitable service delivery, and youth empowerment programs that create meaningful alternatives to radicalization.
- Narratives must be reclaimed: Civil society, religious institutions, and grassroots leaders must counter extremist propaganda by promoting authentic narratives of justice, pluralism, and constructive civic identity.

In a world where extremism feeds on despair, healing must begin with justice. And justice begins by dismantling the entrenched systems of corruption that betray the very people they were meant to protect.

Cross-Border Cooperation and Complicity: Unraveling the Veil of Corruption.

In the complex architecture of global insecurity, corruption operates not merely as an internal affliction but as a transnational lubricant, enabling the seamless expansion of organized crime, narco-terrorism, and extremist networks across borders. At the frontier of this global crisis stands a dangerous paradox: the very agents tasked with defending sovereignty—border officials, customs officers, and law enforcement personnel—are too often compromised, becoming the conduits through which criminal empires thrive.

This is not an accident. It is the strategic weaponization of corruption.

The Machinery of Collusion

Corrupt actors on both sides of national borders collaborate in an intricate web of bribes, coercion, neglect, and silence. Customs agents are paid to look the other way. Intelligence reports are buried. Military patrols are deliberately diverted. Airstrips are left unmonitored. Every act of complicity, no matter how small, represents a betrayal—not just of national duty, but of global security.

In this ecosystem of betrayal:
- Illicit goods move freely, from narcotics and weapons to counterfeit medicine and trafficked persons.
- Financial flows are laundered across jurisdictions, destabilizing economies and funding criminal insurgencies.
- State sovereignty is eroded, replaced by border zones ruled through informal economies, cartel influence, and the iron hand of impunity.

From Local Breach to Global Threat

The consequence is not limited to one nation. The corruption of a single border post in Latin America, Africa, or Southeast Asia can open a corridor for drug trafficking into North America, arms flows into conflict zones, or human trafficking routes into Europe. These are not isolated breaches—they are systemic fractures in the international order.

Transnational criminal organizations operate with the sophistication of multinational corporations—logistics hubs, strategic alliances, decentralized operations. What empowers them is not just violence or ideology, but the corrupted silence of border officials, politicians, and institutional partners across multiple states.

The Failure of Collective Security

Despite countless summits, intergovernmental task forces, and security accords, the infiltration of corruption continues to undermine global cooperation. Intelligence-sharing mechanisms collapse when trust is eroded. Joint task forces disband when internal actors are found complicit. Mutual legal assistance treaties mean little when judicial systems are politicized or purchased.

Thus, corruption is not just a national governance issue—it is a strategic threat to the entire architecture of international law and security cooperation.

Strategic Counter-Offensive: Breaking the Veil

To dismantle this veil of complicity, a paradigm shift is required:

• Zero tolerance must become the standard, not the slogan. International bodies must condition aid, cooperation, and agreements on independently verified anti-corruption benchmarks.

• Cross-border vetting systems must be fortified, ensuring that law enforcement and customs agents undergo continuous evaluation, rotation, and accountability audits.

• International anti-corruption pacts must move from the diplomatic to the operational—creating shared intelligence repositories on corrupt officials, real-time tracking of suspicious financial flows, and collective sanctions mechanisms against complicit networks.

• Civil society and investigative journalism must be protected and empowered as watchdogs, exposing transnational networks that operate in the shadows of state complicity.

Corruption at the border is not a bureaucratic lapse—it is a geopolitical threat vector. As long as money can buy silence at a border post, no wall, drone, or surveillance system will be sufficient. Only through collective moral clarity and institutional courage can we pierce the veil of corruption that enables the global machinery of crime.

Illicit Networks:

Illicit Networks: Unveiling the Nexus of Corruption and Criminality

Illicit networks—whether rooted in narco-terrorism, arms trafficking, or transnational organized crime—do not merely survive in the shadows of state institutions; they often thrive because of them. These networks operate as adaptive, clandestine systems that penetrate political and security infrastructures through a sustained and strategic exploitation of corruption.

From municipal police to customs agencies, from border patrols to senior political figures, these networks rely on a tiered system of complicity. Corrupt officials—coerced, bribed, or ideologically aligned—facilitate trafficking routes, obstruct criminal investigations, and provide real-time intelligence that shields illicit operations. In return, these enablers receive power, protection, and profit—at the expense of public security and state legitimacy.

This symbiosis between corruption and illicit enterprise represents one of the most dangerous nexuses of the 21st century. Corruption is not simply a lubricant for crime; it is the connective tissue of modern criminal systems. It is both a cause and consequence of criminality—fueling terrorist financing, accelerating radicalization, and undermining counterterrorism and law enforcement frameworks from within.

To dismantle these networks, we must recognize that the war against criminality is not fought solely on the battlefield or in the courtroom—it begins within the institutions themselves.

Strategic Responses to a Systemic Threat

A reactive strategy focused on interdictions and arrests is insufficient. What is needed is a holistic offensive grounded in:

• Transparency and Oversight: Establishing robust monitoring mechanisms across law enforcement and judicial sectors to prevent infiltration and detect patterns of corruption.

- Cultural Transformation: Promoting ethics-based leadership and public service integrity through education, internal accountability, and real consequences for betrayal of public duty.
- Structural Reform: Enhancing whistleblower protections, reforming procurement and resource allocation systems, and reducing opportunities for discretionary abuse of power.
- Civil Society Empowerment: Supporting investigative journalism, citizen watchdogs, and non-governmental institutions that expose complicity and hold the state accountable.

Addressing Root Drivers

However, enforcement and institutional reform alone are not enough. Corruption flourishes in contexts marked by:

- Poverty and inequality, where public officials are underpaid and vulnerable to bribery.
- Weak education systems, where civic ethics and public accountability are not prioritized.
- Political apathy or impunity, where justice is selectively applied and transparency is optional.

By confronting these structural deficiencies, governments can weaken the appeal and influence of criminal networks, while restoring trust in democratic institutions and the rule of law.

Illicit networks are not isolated anomalies—they are embedded systems. And like any system, they are vulnerable at their points of connection. By severing their ties to corruption, we strike at the heart of their survival strategy.

Contents

1. THE RISE OF A NARCO-TERRORIST STATE. My Journey as a Counter Narcotics Officer in Venezuela — 1
2. THE NETWORK OF THE SUNS — 28
3. THE EMPIRE EXPANDS. From Revolutionary Discourse to a Systemic Narco-State — 52
4. SEEDS OF SUSPICION. The Birth of a Narco-Terrorist State and Its Hemispheric Expansion — 95
5. CROSSING BORDERS: How the Chavista Narco-Terror Revolution Reached American Soil — 150
6. Conclusion — 176

About the Author — 179

DANGEROUS TIMES. Book Series — 182

Chapter 1
THE RISE OF A NARCO-TERRORIST STATE. My Journey as a Counter Narcotics Officer in Venezuela

Chaos and Orden

"As a society teeters on the edge of collapse, its downfall is heralded not by the roar of war, but by the quiet corrosion of values, the betrayal of justice, and the subjugation of law enforcement to political will and corruption. When a nation's security apparatus becomes entangled in the rot it is meant to resist, it does not merely fail — it turns against its people.

What follows is not just disorder, but moral disintegration. A terrain where criminals thrive, anarchists maneuver, and the righteous are silenced.

These are not distant nightmares. They are lived realities, and I have walked among them."

By Johan Obdola

A Glimpse into Venezuela's Unravelling:

The Role of Law Enforcement, Defence, and Security Officers Before and After the Chavista Revolution.

Venezuela today stands as a harrowing prototype of national collapse—once a relatively stable republic, now a fully operational narco-terrorist state. It is not an anomaly, but a manifestation of a broader and accelerating global trend: the collapse of governance, the rise of authoritarian populism, and the systematic degradation of institutions under the corrosive influence of corruption. Venezuela is both symptom and signal—a warning beacon amidst a growing storm.

Reflecting on my years of service as a counter-narcotics officer in Venezuela, I find myself torn between clarity and anguish. I remember what the country was—its natural abundance, its democratic tradition, its people—and am haunted by what it has become. The frustration never fades. It simmers beneath the surface of every memory.

How does a nation endowed with immense oil wealth, ecological riches, and geopolitical influence descend into a lawless stronghold for criminal cartels, terrorist organizations, and kleptocratic rulers? The answer lies in a lethal convergence: foreign influence, radical ideology, and internal rot—especially the metastasis of corruption, the mother of all systemic evils.

At the heart of Venezuela's disintegration was a deliberate strategy. Aided by international actors, cloaked in the language of populism, and rooted in a culture of impunity, the Chavista revolution weaponized poverty, identity, and resentment. What followed was not accidental—it was the construction of a criminal state apparatus: sophisticated, ideological, violent, and globally connected.

The country's transformation into a narco-terrorist state was gradual, calculated, and is still unfolding. This metamorphosis has involved the strategic co-option of the military, intelligence, law enforcement, and judicial systems—eroding any line between public service and criminal enterprise. The State, as a governing institution, has been hollowed out and replaced by a cartel-led structure of power, guided not by the constitution but by the ruthless imperatives of regime survival and geopolitical alignment with the enemies of the West.

Today, Venezuela functions as a global hub for illicit operations. It is a launchpad for terrorism, espionage, trafficking, and ideological subversion. Iran's Quds Force, Russia's GRU and Wagner Group, and Chinese surveillance interests all intersect on Venezuelan soil, sheltered by the regime's open hostility toward the United States, Canada, and democratic allies across Latin America and Europe.

What was once Latin America's most promising democracy is now a model of hybrid warfare against civil society, truth, and order. It is a geopolitical fulcrum in the hands of rogue regimes and a playground for globalized crime. The regime's criminalized hierarchy thrives on dirty money, the exploitation of human suffering, and the silencing of dissent through psychological and physical terror. Venezuelan territory is now a battlefield without declaration—a frontline in the war against democratic civilization.

Even amid ongoing presidential negotiations—often flaunted before international observers as democratic overtures—the true objectives remain unaltered: securing impunity for crimes against humanity, laundering vast sums of stolen public wealth, and sustaining strategic pressure against the liberal international order.

The regime's hierarchy is pyramidal, militarized, and deeply infiltrated by transnational criminal networks. Its foundations are built on the complicity of law enforcement, security forces, and political operators who long ago abandoned the constitution for personal enrichment and ideological dogma.

Venezuela's collapse was not an isolated implosion; it was engineered. And it continues to metastasize. Today, nations such as Nicaragua and Bolivia, and those orbiting the Bolivarian ideological axis, are replicating the same model—state-sanctioned criminality, populist radicalization, and kleptocratic violence. Behind the curtain stands Cuba, the ideological architect and strategic mentor of this revolution—a regime that turned Venezuela into a satellite laboratory of destruction.

The implications are no longer regional. Venezuela is not simply a failed state. It is a hostile platform, generating real-time threats to global security: narco-financed terrorism, migration crises, proxy warfare, and hybrid infiltration. It is a bellwether of the world to come if corruption is left unchecked and if impunity becomes normalized.

This chapter, this testimony, is not just about Venezuela. It is about the anatomy of collapse and the lessons we must learn before more nations fall into the abyss.

The Subversion of Security: From Institutions of Protection to Engines of Oppression

To understand Venezuela's current condition, one must dissect the transformation from a nation—imperfect but striving—into an absurd and criminal simulacrum of statehood. This is not merely a story of institutional collapse. It is the story of deliberate deconstruction, where governance, law, and public trust were replaced with survivalism, terror, and systemic crime.

What was once a land of relative order and institutional pride is now a distorted theatre of contradictions—where logic is mocked, where absurdity governs, and where the surreal becomes the daily norm.

At the center of this collapse lies the metamorphosis of the nation's police, security, and military apparatus—entities once tasked with safeguarding the people, now functioning as armed subsidiaries of a narco-criminal regime. They are no longer protectors; they are instruments of control, tools of repression, and beneficiaries of impunity.

Before the rise of Chavismo, Venezuela could count on a law enforcement system rooted in professionalism. National, state, and municipal police forces—though not without flaws—had trained officers, standards of recruitment, and a growing culture of academic advancement. Some units even earned international recognition. The armed forces, in turn, were a source of national dignity—an institution committed to sovereignty and constitutional mandate, with a clear chain of command and discipline.

At that time, Colombian cartels were only beginning to penetrate Venezuelan territory. The "Cartel de los Soles", formed by high-ranking officers of the National Guard, became the first conduit for criminal collaboration. Through this channel, Colombian and later Mexican cartels (notably Cartel de Sinaloa) secured operational partnerships with Venezuelan actors, effectively initiating the nation's transition into a narco-state.

The Chavista revolution did not just accelerate this process—it institutionalized it.

With Chávez's arrival, the regime opened the gates wide to transnational criminal infiltration. What followed was not chaos born of mismanagement—it was a strategic offering of Venezuela to geopolitical adversaries: Iran, Russia, China, and criminal networks worldwide. The result was a nation held hostage by both foreign agendas and internal treason.

The professionalization efforts within Venezuela's security sector were systematically dismantled. Police institutions that once demanded university degrees, training academies, and continuing education were hollowed out. Salaries stagnated. Corruption flourished. Loyalty to ideology replaced qualifications.

The armed forces—once protected by decent pay, retirement security, and constitutional mission—were similarly undermined. The only comparable class in Venezuelan public life was the PDVSA elite, but even this was co-opted into the regime's criminal ecosystem.

What emerged was a perverse pyramid of command, where each Chavista leader—often a civilian-turned-commandante—oversaw a criminal micro-state composed of hand-picked generals, police chiefs, prosecutors, and armed gangs. These networks operated in parallel to the state, but with state resources, uniforms, and full impunity.

The regime's armed enforcers, the "Colectivos", took to the streets—not as police, but as political shock troops. They acted as executioners, spies, enforcers, and extortionists. These paramilitary units, openly armed by the state, merged with urban criminal gangs and were tasked with policing dissent, crushing protests, and safeguarding regime assets.

In this new ecosystem, security became criminalized, and crime became legalized—as long as it served the revolution.

The mutation was ideological. It was institutional. It was complete.

What had once been a process of institutional development—the slow but meaningful professionalization of security and defense—was reversed in record time. Under the Bolivarian Revolution, military and police institutions were no longer the republic's guardians; they became the revolutionary arm of a criminal regime.

The emergence of an ideological doctrine, embedded within military and police structures, ensured that the very notion of "public security" was redefined. The function of security shifted from serving the citizenry to serving the revolution. Law enforcement now meant political repression. Defense meant regime protection. Crime fighting became a selective practice: it punished enemies, not crimes.

This ideological alignment went beyond doctrine. It permeated the mission, the uniforms, the oaths, and the daily operations of those sworn to protect. The fusion of ideology with force birthed a hybrid security system—one that defends corruption, traffics influence, and crushes any form of organized resistance.

From the outside, this may seem irrational. But within the logic of Chavismo, it is tragically effective. The revolution knew that no authoritarian system can survive unless it controls the security sector. So, it dismantled the one Venezuela had—and rebuilt it in its own criminal image.

This transformation was not symbolic; it was operational.

Security forces became revenue-generating machines. They trafficked fuel, food, weapons, and people. They provided protection to drug convoys. They managed illegal gold and diamond extractions. They enforced black market monopolies. They brokered political persecution. And they silenced anyone who dared to expose them.

The Bolivarian security doctrine was never about national defense. It was always about revolutionary survival—and survival required terror, infiltration, and corruption as policy.

As I reflect on this transformation, I am haunted by a personal truth: I narrowly escaped becoming either a participant—or a casualty—of this criminal order.

Had I stayed in Venezuela, I might have been forced to comply, silenced by complicity, or eliminated for resisting. I left the country as a refugee before the full imposition of the Chavista regime. It was a painful decision. But looking back, I understand it was one of life or death.

The Law Enforcement Dilemma.

Operating on the Edge of Sovereignty, Survival, and Subversion

Delta Amacuro—also known as Delta del Orinoco—is a region of immense ecological richness, geopolitical complexity, and strategic vulnerability. Bordered by the Atlantic Ocean to the northeast, Guyana to the southeast, and the Venezuelan states of Bolívar and Monagas to the south and west, it stands at the intersection of some of South America's most crucial and contested territories.

As Director of Counter-Narcotics Operations for the region, my area of responsibility extended beyond the formal boundaries of Delta Amacuro. It encompassed operations throughout Sucre, Bolívar, and Monagas, often requiring coordination across inter-jurisdictional lines and politically sensitive zones. These were not abstract missions—they were urgent, high-risk operations in a region overrun by illicit flows and institutional decay.

Among the most critical of these was the strategic coastal corridor facing Trinidad and Tobago, the southernmost island nation in the Caribbean. Just east of us lay El Esequibo, the vast 159,000 km² territory long disputed with Guyana. This territorial contention—ignored by many—served as fertile ground for trafficking operations, black-market trade, and unregulated movement. For the transnational narco-networks operating in the shadows of crumbling sovereignty, this was not a conflict zone—it was an open corridor.

I led counter-narcotics patrols deep into the rivers, mangroves, and jungle trails—regions not only governed by nature but by silence, fear, and shadow power. With a trusted military-police task force, I commanded coordinated riverine and maritime patrols that traversed these zones with methodical precision. Each sortie brought us face-to-face with traffickers, guerrilla couriers, corrupt intermediaries, and occasionally—agents of foreign intelligence.

One of the areas that most tested our tactical capabilities and ethical fortitude was Antonio Díaz municipality, an epicenter of jungle terrain, coastal routes, and ancestral Warao communities. These Indigenous groups, living alongside Creole families engaged in subsistence hunting and fishing, were the quiet witnesses—and sometimes collateral victims—of a growing underworld economy that trafficked more than cocaine: it trafficked power, terror, and silence.

It was within this volatile configuration that I began to receive consistent intelligence reports about fast-boat narcotics shipments to Trinidad and Tobago. These weren't rumors. They were tactical indicators confirmed by reconnaissance, surveillance logs, and direct intel from T&T counterparts, with whom we had established informal but strategic channels of communication. A complex maritime corridor—bypassing formal naval scrutiny—had emerged, transforming Delta Amacuro into a launchpad for international drug exports.

The dilemma: pursue them across disputed waters—or stand down and risk complicity by omission.

After days of analysis and covert observation, I convened with my intelligence deputy chief, Nerio Montañez, a professional I trusted with both judgment and survival. We decided to deploy deep into the Esequibo frontier, near the zone known as La Línea. This was no ordinary patrol. It was an intentional penetration into disputed and sensitive territory—a tripwire mission blending intelligence collection, operational deterrence, and direct confrontation with the unseen operators who believed they owned that sea.

From the Warao village of Guayo, Nerio and I launched the mission aboard a Balajú-style patrol boat, outfitted with twin 150HP outboard motors. Nerio carried a rifle, two sidearms, a military radio, and essential provisions. Our crew remained behind, preparing food and maintaining contact protocols. The objective was both reconnaissance and presence. We needed to demonstrate—both to criminals and potential observers—that Venezuela's officers still had a line to hold.

For nearly two hours, we maneuvered through shifting currents, narrow tributaries, and open ocean sprays. As we reached La Línea, where the jungle breathes salt and the sea drinks shadow, we found an elevated vantage point to observe the area. The region's haunting beauty clashed with the grim knowledge of what passed through it: drug convoys, smuggling routes, and geopolitical whispers carried by foreign agents, criminal syndicates, and regional power brokers.

Roughly twenty-five minutes after establishing position, a vessel approached.

Coincidence? Absolutely not. We were already being watched.

A lone figure on board raised his hand in greeting. His voice cut through the stillness:

"Señor Johan, this is a gift from my master."

In that moment, it became clear. This wasn't merely a field operation. It was a message—and a warning.

The Offer That Echoed in the Delta

In response to the unexpected arrival of the lone vessel, I signaled Nerio to maintain his stance. Trained for exactly this type of confrontation, he remained motionless, his FAL rifle steady, eyes scanning the jungle flanks and riverbanks for hidden movements. The air was humid and electrically still, the type of silence that only came before an ambush—or a proposal.

I stepped forward, my Glock .40 raised at chest level, angled slightly downward but ready. Calm, measured, alert.

"Identify yourself and your sender," I ordered.

The man, dressed in civilian clothing but wearing an unmistakable aura of submission and coded authority, stood at the bow of his balajú—a vessel favored by local traffickers for its speed and stealth. He raised his hand in a peace gesture.

"Señor Johan, this is a gift from my master," he called out in a respectful, almost trembling voice.

Then, lifting a black waterproof duffel bag, he added:

"My master Ceferino sends you a gift. It's seven hundred thousand dollars in cash—for you, señor Johan."

His face betrayed a mixture of fear and duty. "Please, accept it," he insisted, "I can't go back and tell my master you refused."

It wasn't the first time the name Ceferino had crossed my desk—or my path.

He was a rising local narco-operator, once a low-level intermediary with modest routes in Monagas, but who, by then, had begun consolidating power across Delta Amacuro. Intelligence reports linked him directly to emissaries of the Cali cartel, using Venezuelan river networks and jungle trails to transport shipments north toward the Caribbean and east through Guyana and Suriname. The rise of Ceferino exemplified how quickly localized criminal actors could evolve into transnational assets—when the state either turned a blind eye or offered open doors.

Weeks prior, in a secure strategic meeting with Nerio and Commissioner Lino, two of the most respected officers I knew from DISIP (the Directorate of Intelligence and Prevention Services), I had outlined operational deployments with extreme discretion. Given the escalating infiltration of military and police officials by narco-networks, we deliberately withheld key mission details—even from supposedly secure command posts. Ceferino's growing interest in our operations, and his attempts to corrupt our ranks, had been a focal point of that conversation.

I looked at the bag. I did not need to open it. I had seen that kind of money before—in seizures, in bribes offered to others, and once, years earlier, in a courtroom exhibit sealed in plastic. But this was different. It was being offered to me. On a beach. In disputed waters. By a man who may or may not have been alone.

"Ceferino sends me this money?" I asked flatly, concealing the tension behind a mask of detached inquiry.

The man nodded quickly, anxiously. "Yes, señor. He says he respects you. That it's better if you work together. That this is... just the beginning."

My decision came without hesitation. But it had to be delivered with both clarity and authority.

"You're in trouble, man," I said, slowly. "Take your money. Tell your master that I don't accept gifts, and he already knows it."

I stepped forward, handed the bag back without touching its contents.

"Go back to him before I change my mind and arrest you."

The man froze. His eyes widened. "I can't go back empty-handed. Please, señor Johan. I can't."

In that instant, Nerio, who had remained disciplined but visibly agitated by the prolonged standoff, stepped forward and raised his Beretta 9mm, pressing it beside the man's right ear. The shot was deliberate, a warning more than an execution—but a violent one. The bullet discharged a few centimetres from the ear canal, producing a sharp concussion wave that ripped into the man's equilibrium.

The man screamed, staggered, and fell to his knees. A thin line of blood trickled from his ear. Temporary deafness and acute vertigo would follow—a standard technique in psychological warfare, known to us but horrifying to the uninitiated.

Without saying a word, Nerio helped the man regain his footing. He retrieved the bag, placed it back on the balajú, and nudged the vessel away from the shore with his foot. I watched every movement, still scanning the treeline, half expecting retaliation.

The man, still shaking, started the engine. His eyes no longer pleaded—they begged for escape. He turned the boat around and disappeared slowly into the mouth of the river, toward the open sea.

The jungle fell silent again. But the air had changed.

That moment crystallized the existential dilemma of law enforcement in Venezuela's eastern frontiers: to stand firm and risk your life—or bend, and become part of the machinery you once swore to dismantle. What Ceferino attempted was not unique. It had become common practice across the criminal pyramid that governed Venezuela, where narco-captains served as patrons of mayors, judges, and military colonels.

Some of these men wore uniforms. Others wore suits. Many wore both.

The system rewarded those who complied and crushed those who resisted. Those who resisted—like me, like Nerio—knew there would be a cost. Perhaps not immediately. But eventually. These decisions, taken in the heat of a tropical sun with a rifle trained on an emissary, were remembered. Recorded. Passed on.

This was not the first time I was offered a bribe. It was certainly not the last.

But it was perhaps the moment I knew that no law enforcement mission in Venezuela was isolated from the corrupt architecture of impunity now embedded in every corridor of power. The cartels had learned that the state was not their enemy—it was their host.

From that day forward, my badge became a target, not a shield. But I had already made peace with that.

Because if one officer doesn't say no—no one will.

Do you have the Guts to Lead the Fight Against Drug Cartels?

When Armando Salazar, one of the few honest and courageous political leaders I have ever met, took office as Governor of Delta Amacuro, he summoned me to his office without ceremony. The room was quiet. He looked me in the eye and asked a question that would define the course of my life:

"Johan, do you have the guts to lead the fight against the cartels ?"

I didn't need time to answer. He already knew I did.

Governor Salazar was a man who understood what it meant to face death for principle. Though controversial, he had earned a reputation for his uncompromising stance against corruption and drug trafficking—twin forces suffocating the Delta Amacuro region and devastating the already fragile Warao Indigenous communities, who lived along the rivers and in the deep jungle. He had studied my record—my work dismantling criminal operations across several Venezuelan states—and he saw in me not just a law enforcement officer, but an ally in the existential war for Venezuela's soul.

With no ceremony, he appointed me Chief of Counter-Narcotics for the entire state.

I accepted the position knowing it would put my life and the lives of my team in constant danger. But I also knew the stakes: either we pushed back the cartels, or we surrendered the region completely to their control.

War on a $25,000 Budget

Our resources were laughably limited.

I was handed an annual budget of just $25,000 USD. With this, I had to cover operations, intelligence, logistics, and basic personnel expenses. But what we lacked in funding, we made up for in determination.

I assembled a compact but highly motivated team:
- An administrative unit: a trusted lawyer, an operations administrator, and a small support staff.
- An operational task force: 50 men and women drawn from the Delta Amacuro State Police, bolstered by elements of the Army, agents from the DISIP intelligence service, and, occasionally, support from the National Guard.

We launched an aggressive campaign of riverine and jungle operations, paired with continuous urban presence. We established outposts, intelligence nodes, and surveillance points in strategic locations throughout the state. Simultaneously, we initiated a parallel, covert intelligence operation aimed at mapping the depth of cartel penetration and exposing their enablers within our own institutions.

What we uncovered was more horrifying than I had feared.

The Invisible Empire: Corruption Unmasked

Through deep infiltration, wiretaps, HUMINT reports, and cooperation with external intelligence sources—including allies in Trinidad and Tobago and unofficial counterparts in Colombia—we discovered a sobering reality: the narco-structure had already metastasized.

Judges, public prosecutors, senior police commanders, military officers, customs agents, and even members of the intelligence community were either already on cartel payrolls—or negotiating their entry.

The Colombian cartels, especially Cali, had gone beyond infiltration. They were now embedding themselves within the political and economic landscape of eastern Venezuela.

- They purchased farms, fishing companies, and jungle properties at prices well above market value to create logistical and financial camouflage.
- Property prices in Delta Amacuro, Sucre, Monagas, and Bolívar spiked without economic explanation.
- Known cartel members—some of whom were fugitives in Colombia—began appearing openly at private events, business meetings, and even in state-sponsored gatherings.

These weren't rumors. They were patterns. Verified, confirmed, mapped.

Based on corroborated intelligence, I estimated that between 200 and 300 metric tons of cocaine were leaving Delta Amacuro's shores annually—headed toward Trinidad and Tobago, and then distributed to the Caribbean, Europe, and North America.

Rebuilding Integrity—From the Inside

Faced with this systemic rot, I had to make an early strategic decision: rebuild morale and loyalty within my own ranks before confronting the enemy outside.

I implemented internal protocols to protect and motivate our operational teams. I instituted informal rotation policies to avoid burnout, incentivized integrity, and created non-monetary recognition frameworks—from internal commendations to direct meetings with the governor for those who performed exemplary duties.

At the same time, I launched public-facing initiatives: civic forums, school visits, and radio broadcasts that subtly raised awareness about the drug trade, corruption, and the danger of silence. These were not propaganda—they were preventive countermeasures designed to build resistance within the population, particularly in Warao communities being exploited by both traffickers and complicit officials.

Governor Salazar gave me his full support.

"Start wherever you need. But don't hold back," he said.

There Are No Half-Measures in War

I knew the risk. We weren't just fighting criminals—we were fighting a narco-political system that wore the mask of the Republic.

This was not just about policing. It was about reclaiming sovereignty from a network that had corrupted institutions, language, and reality itself. The drug cartels didn't operate in shadows—they operated from state buildings, behind press conferences, and inside uniforms.

I wasn't naïve. I knew that our days were numbered if we weren't fully committed. There were only two paths in this war:
1. You fight.
2. Or you're already compromised.

There is no middle ground.

We chose to fight.

I Was In—And So Was the War

I was in.

There was no turning back. And if I was all in, then everyone under my command had to be, too. There was no room for ambiguity. No margin for compromise. I convened my core leadership team and laid out the new paradigm: we would open every front—operational, informational, covert, strategic, and alternative. This was not just a tactical fight. It was a systemic war.

I designed a multi-pronged framework:
- Public Awareness: Campaigns to inform the population—especially in indigenous and remote areas—about the nature and consequences of the cartel operations. We crafted messaging to build resistance from below.
- Operational Deployment: I established rotating squads for jungle, riverine, and urban missions, preventing burnout and maintaining tactical unpredictability.
- Compartmentalized Intelligence: We created autonomous intel cells, often integrating vetted officers from outside Delta Amacuro, limiting information exposure and reducing the risk of leaks.
- Allied Civilian Networks: I quietly enlisted the help of lawyers, journalists, accountants, and retired police and military professionals. Some acted as informal advisors. Others served as intelligence feeders.

But the scale of the threat demanded more than regional coordination.

A Strategic Risk: Engaging the United States

Understanding the rapid escalation of narco-criminal power—and the deep institutional corruption that shielded it—I made the strategic decision to establish contact with the U.S. Embassy in Caracas, focusing on collaboration with:

- DEA (Drug Enforcement Administration)
- FBI (Federal Bureau of Investigation)
- U.S. Military Attachés (including SOUTHCOM)
- And informally, with German police liaisons posted at the European embassies.

This was not a casual alliance. It was a calculated geopolitical move, and I knew it came with risks. But it also marked a turning point.

We began receiving direct intelligence support, regional data analysis, satellite insights, and counter-narcotics training. The DEA, in particular, became an invaluable strategic partner. Through their assistance, we were able to trace drug flows, identify mid-level operators, and better understand the evolving role of Delta Amacuro as a key maritime corridor in the international cocaine trade.

It was no longer a local problem.

It was a hemispheric threat, and our office had become a frontline command post in that battle.

Success Brings Enemies

As our operations gained traction, the impact became tangible—and so did the consequences.
- Seizures increased.
- Routes were exposed.
- Local and foreign media began covering our work.
- I gave interviews to national newspapers and TV stations, and welcomed foreign correspondents seeking insight into Venezuela's emerging status as a narco-hub.

Publicly, I became a symbol of resistance.

But privately, I was now marked.

Within weeks, threats began pouring in. Death threats. Kidnapping threats. Surveillance against my family. Covert intimidation against my staff. It wasn't coming from the jungle. It was coming from offices in Caracas.

Officials whose faces I had shaken hands with. Men in suits who had praised my work in public—and plotted my removal in private.

I knew what was happening.

I was hitting too hard, too fast. And I wasn't for sale.

Expanding the Shield

To sustain momentum and shield my operations from betrayal, I made another bold move.

I met with senior officers from the Venezuelan Navy and Air Force—the branches of the military that had, at the time, remained the least penetrated by narco-corruption. They understood the gravity of the situation and quietly assigned me an elite rapid response and intelligence unit that would operate independently from my main task force, using different protocols and reporting lines.

This team became our surgical spear—capable of executing high-risk operations in real time, including interdicting cocaine convoys on the river, surveilling air routes, and conducting nighttime raids on jungle camps.

Our combined forces delivered concrete results:
- Hundreds of tons of cocaine were seized over several months.
- Key nodes in the cartel networks—drivers, local liaisons, dock managers, even judicial collaborators—were identified.
- Cross-border intel-sharing with Trinidad and Tobago, Colombia, and the United States intensified.

But something was changing.

The Scale of the Enemy

Despite the arrests, the seizures, and the network disruptions, I began to observe a pattern:
- The flow of drugs was not decreasing.
- Instead, new actors emerged quickly.
- Properties acquired by traffickers increased.
- Cartel-linked businesses flourished.

I wasn't dealing with infiltration.

I was dealing with occupation.

The narco-state had matured. It was no longer just a parasite within the Venezuelan system—it was becoming the system itself.

It dawned on me that we were winning battles, but losing the war.

Fighting Alone

Despite continued contact with the Ministries of Interior and Defense—and my attempts to keep senior officials informed through detailed operational reports—I began to sense growing silence from Caracas. The same men who once praised my efforts now avoided direct engagement.

So I doubled down on public visibility. I coordinated interviews, press briefings, and documentaries. I released carefully curated intelligence findings that pointed to the estimated 300 to 500 metric tons of cocaine departing annually from Delta Amacuro alone.

The press became an extension of our resistance.

I wasn't looking for fame. I was fighting to survive—and to give the truth a place to breathe in a country increasingly built on lies.

The reaction was swift.

International experts began requesting access to our operations. NGO observers submitted reports to foreign embassies. Human rights groups started connecting the dots between narco-trafficking, Indigenous exploitation, and systemic repression.

But back home, the pressure escalated.

The Enemy Conceals Its Fangs—But Delivers Deadly Bites

By mid-2004, the signs of imminent escalation became undeniable.

According to intelligence I received through both formal channels and trusted operatives embedded in Caracas and the eastern states, decisions had been made—decisions to eliminate me. Not just me, but also members of my operational and intelligence teams, as well as civilian collaborators who had lent their skills to our mission. The death threats were no longer abstract. The information was consistent, credible, and chilling in its clarity.

It was clear: the enemy was no longer just watching. It was now hunting.

In response, I activated a comprehensive threat mitigation plan—a multidimensional protocol to anticipate and counteract potential attacks. It included:
- Tactical rotations of my staff and operatives.
- Secured communications and movement protocols.
- Heightened family security measures.
- Strategic disengagement from predictable routines.

And, above all, a clear directive to continue operations at full speed.

This was not a time to retreat. It was a time to confront the shadow.

First Shots Fired: A Direct Hit

The first two assassination attempts came swiftly—contract killings ordered by high-level actors embedded within the very institutions meant to uphold the law.

Both failed.

Each resulted in armed confrontations, and I emerged physically unscathed. But the message was clear.

Weeks later, during an engagement on the maritime fringe of the Delta's jungle coastline, the third attack came—not through an ambush, but in open confrontation. A high-velocity round tore through my right leg during a pursuit operation against cartel boats in the Orinoco Delta.

I remember it vividly. We were in full pursuit aboard our "Balajú," its twin 150HP engines roaring as we closed in on two cartel vessels weaving through the muddy waters. Bullets sliced through the humid air. Then—impact. A burning sensation surged through my leg, followed by pain so sharp it almost blinded me.

Despite the wound, I ordered the pursuit to continue. Two of the cartel operatives were hit and plunged into the current. We never recovered the bodies—the river claimed them.

Our boat had only a rudimentary medical kit. One of my men, a combat medic in a past life, wrapped the wound tightly and reached for the emergency bottle of brandy I kept for cold nights. We sterilized. I drank. The pain blurred with adrenaline. Nearly an hour later, an army helicopter landed on a narrow patch of jungle clearing and flew me to Tucupita Hospital. The wound was deep, but I had survived—again.

The war had changed.

A Silence Marked by Death

Only days after my recovery, tragedy struck harder.

On September 1st, 2004, journalist Mauro Marcano—a friend, ally, and fearless investigator—was murdered outside his apartment. He had been working closely with me on a series of reports about drug kingpins in eastern Venezuela, especially the Cartel del Sol—now infamously known as Cartel de los Soles, a criminal network embedded within the Venezuelan military and political apparatus.

Mauro had warned the public. He had named names. He had published too many truths. And for that, he was silenced.

He wasn't just a journalist. Mauro was also the brother of José "Tucupita" Marcano, a Major League Baseball infielder. His death made ripples across sports and political communities—but within the inner circles of intelligence, we knew what it meant: a warning.

Shortly after Mauro's assassination, my trusted field agent Rodolfo Aurea was ambushed and killed. The message delivered through intermediaries was not subtle:

"You're next."

The spiral continued. Months later, the commander of the Delta Amacuro State Police died in what was officially labelled a "traffic accident." The investigation was perfunctory. The case was closed within days. Evidence was buried—literally and institutionally.

The message had now become policy.

The Final Realization

It was now undeniable: I was living and operating under siege.

- Enemies wore uniforms.
- Courthouses protected traffickers.
- Colleagues disappeared or were executed.

And yet, despite every threat, every ambush, and every betrayal, I still had one decision to make.

Would I disappear in silence, or strike one final blow?

I knew I could not stop the machine. Not alone. But I could document it. Expose it. Leave behind a trail—a record for history, for justice, for the future.

The time for hesitation was over. I would make my last move, on my terms.

Even if it meant becoming a target not only of the cartels—but of the very nation I had sworn to protect.

A Final Decision at the Edge of Collapse

I found myself compelled—no, morally obligated—to raise the alarm.

What had begun as isolated skirmishes in jungle corridors and riverine routes had now escalated into a national metastasis: Colombia's drug cartels, emboldened by impunity and armed with unimaginable capital, were no longer mere external actors. They had become internal architects of decay. Their infiltration spread beyond border towns and forgotten provinces, penetrating the nerve centers of power—government, military, judiciary, intelligence, and the private sector alike.

The signs were no longer subtle. The assault was not only systemic—it was surgical.

Corruption, once a byproduct of weak governance, had now become a central operating principle. Intelligence agencies were manipulated, military command structures co-opted, public prosecutors silenced. Entire provinces became narco-administered zones, where justice was bought, silence was enforced, and loyalty was traded in kilos.

And in the face of this encroaching darkness, I came to a singular realization:

No one else was coming.

There would be no cavalry, no final order from above, no strategic coalition of integrity waiting to be activated. The institutions that once trained me, protected me, and empowered me to lead—were now the very targets of subversion or already fallen to it.

This was no longer just a professional war. It was existential.

A Leader's Burden, A Nation's Crisis

The decision to act—to confront rather than accommodate, to expose rather than retreat—was not just born of strategy. It was a choice rooted in conscience.

I understood fully the cost of that choice.

To stand firm in the eye of the storm was to become a lightning rod—not only for criminal syndicates, but also for the politicians, judges, and generals who had grown accustomed to the comforts of complicity. My presence, my voice, my work—they became threats in themselves.

But if the cartels had succeeded in anything, it was in awakening my deepest conviction:

That a nation cannot remain a nation when its institutions become instruments of organized crime.

If Venezuela was to have any future—if any child in Delta Amacuro or any officer still loyal to their oath was to believe in that future—someone had to stand the line. Someone had to build resistance within the collapse. Not as a martyr. But as a witness. As a fighter. As a living record.

This Story Begins Where Silence Ends

This chapter closes not with triumph, but with resolve.

I made the decision to act—not with arrogance, but with clarity. Not in search of personal glory, but to shield what remained of a disintegrating republic. What followed were events few have lived to tell. Operations, betrayals, near-death moments, allies fallen, institutions exposed—and above all, a truth so unfiltered, it threatened to unravel the false stability projected to the world.

As the next pages unfold, you, the reader, will walk through the underbelly of a nation in transformation—from fragile democracy to a narco-criminal state. You will witness not only the strategic architecture of a criminal empire, but the human cost of those who chose to resist it.

This is a story of infiltration and defiance. Of collapse and courage. Of solitude and moral clarity.

Above all, it is a testimony.

A testimony not just to what I witnessed, but to what I was willing to do—when doing nothing would have meant complicity.

Let the record begin.

Chapter 2
THE NETWORK OF THE SUNS

Shadows Unveiled

By Johan Obdola

In shadows deep where darkness weaves,
A realm obscured, where deceit conceives.
Whispers linger, a clandestine choir,
Enemies of humanity, fueling the fire.

Beneath the surface, a covert dance,
A world entangled in a dangerous trance.
Cloaked in secrecy, their faces veiled,
Masters of deception, their schemes unveiled.

Through corridors of power, they silently tread,
Aiming arrows at the heart, where trust has bled.
Within the folds of society, they find their way,
Enemies unseen, casting shadows gray.

But in the realm where truth takes flight,
A champion rises to dispel the night.
Exposing foes with courage and might,
The defender emerges, a beacon of light.

Through the chapters of a relentless quest,
To reveal the enemy's covert nest.
In the dance of shadows, a truth unfolds,
A tale of defiance that history holds.

With every word, the veil unravels,
Exposing the enemies and their dark travels.
In the echoes of exposure, a victory's spun,

A saga of justice, where battles are won.

To the enemies of humanity, laid bare,
In the sunlight, your secrets we declare.
For in the pages of truth, we now inscribe,
The names of those who sought to divide.

This is the reckoning—
And the light will not be denied.

Exposing the Enemies. Between Death and Denunciation

After surviving multiple assassination attempts and painfully witnessing the deaths of loyal men under my command, I reached a decisive turning point. The reality was undeniable: criminal power had metastasized far beyond isolated gangs or rogue actors—it now coursed through the veins of the Venezuelan state itself.

The battle I was waging could no longer be contained in the field. It had to reach desks, chambers, and institutional archives. And so I shifted strategy.

I initiated a chain of official communications addressed directly to governors, mayors, judges, and top officials from the ministries, armed forces, and intelligence services. The names listed in those communications were not vague references. They were known actors—individuals for whom I had collected evidence of complicity with narco-trafficking organizations. These were not just warnings—they were accusations backed by classified reports and field intelligence. My communications exposed a systemic web of criminal infiltration: assassinations of public servants, sabotaged operations, and the active dismantling of the state's internal integrity.

At the same time, I maintained constant, discreet communications with agents from the U.S. Drug Enforcement Administration (DEA) at the American Embassy in Caracas. I also engaged with intelligence liaisons from the United Kingdom, Germany, and Spain—nations that still harbored a strategic interest in countering drug cartels in Latin America. Despite Venezuela's rapidly fraying ties with the international community, these operatives were still listening. Some even acted.

I was aware that each message sent, each report signed, each agency alerted, placed me more deeply in the crosshairs of those who no longer distinguished between political rivalry and mortal threat. But I could not remain silent.

And then came the visit.

The Visit from the Generals

It was a warm, quiet afternoon in my office. I was receiving a small delegation of Warao Indigenous leaders who had traveled for hours by river to meet with me—community elders seeking protection and representation in a country increasingly deaf to their suffering.

Without warning, my secretary entered, visibly unsettled.

"Commander," she said, "a commission of high-ranking National Guard officers has arrived... led by the Second General Commander himself."

Her voice was strained. These were men who didn't knock.

Their intention was clear. Rank demanded submission. Presence implied threat.

I didn't flinch.

"Let them wait," I replied. "These Indigenous leaders made a long journey to be heard. They have my full attention."

I instructed her to offer the officers water, coffee, and protocol. Then I returned calmly to the meeting, honoring the dignity of those who had no battalions—only broken trust.

Minutes later, my secretary returned.

"They left," she said bluntly. "And they are not happy."

I nodded. Their discontent was anticipated. Their presence was never about courtesy. It was a warning.

Not long after, the call came. It was Governor Armando Salazar, sharp and irate.

"What the fuck is wrong with you?" he snapped.

I let him speak.

"That was the Second General Commander. He came directly from Caracas with a special commission. They came to question you about your testimony in Congress. And you made them wait?"

"Armando," I replied evenly, "you know I was in a formal meeting. These men believe their uniforms give them the right to barge into an office without notice and demand instant submission. I won't participate in that theatre."

I paused, then delivered the deeper message.

"And you know who they are."

He didn't answer.

"They came as envoys," I said. "But not from the government—from the Cartel del Sol. And you know it."

A long silence followed.

"We'll talk later," he finally muttered, then hung up.

But the real confrontation was still to come.

Later that day, I was summoned to the Regional Command of the National Guard. I knew exactly what to expect. The room I walked into was thick with hostility—officers in full dress uniform, warship arrogance on display, their eyes burning with fury and entitlement.

They didn't ask questions. They launched insults.

"You're a disgrace," one spat.

"You've created a national security crisis."

"You're just an Indian," sneered another—using the term with the venom of colonial contempt.

I listened, in silence, unmoved. I had been hunted by cartels. I had buried men braver than these uniformed cowards. Their voices did not shake me.

When they finally quieted, expecting an apology or submission, I stood and addressed the most senior general in the room.

"Have you finished your intimidation mission?" I asked calmly. "It won't work."

I looked him in the eyes.

"If anything happens to me, there are records—documents, statements, and testimonies. Many people already have them. And General... we both know whose message you're delivering."

A pause.

"Perhaps your real bosses. Perhaps your colleagues from the suns."

Then I turned and left.

Cartel del Sol. Cartel de los Soles.

Before Chávez, it was called the Cartel del Sol, a shadow power structure within the National Guard. After the revolution, it became the Cartel de los Soles—a syndicate controlled by high-ranking regime officials, embedded into the very core of the Venezuelan military and state. What began as institutional corruption metastasized into full-scale narco-governance.

That day, in that room, I wasn't just facing military men—I was confronting a criminal state in uniform.

A Country in Narco-Collapse

As the grip of the cartels tightened around Venezuela's institutions, the signs of national disintegration became impossible to ignore. What had once been isolated episodes of violence or corruption transformed into a fully integrated system of narco-governance—braiding together military uniforms, judicial robes, and ministerial offices with the invisible chains of drug money and impunity.

Despite maintaining open channels of coordination with the U.S. Drug Enforcement Administration (DEA), as well as liaison officers from the United Kingdom, Germany, and Spain, I watched with growing alarm as the tide of criminality surged far beyond what even our worst-case projections had imagined. Cartels from Colombia—seasoned, violent, and transnational—were no longer just infiltrating Venezuela. They were embedding, rooting, and ruling.

The country's coastal regions—especially key ports and airport terminals—became primary vectors of illicit commerce. Cocaine trafficking intensified not only through traditional routes, but also via river networks and clandestine airstrips deep in the jungle. What began as corruption metastasized into strategic territorial control.

At the same time, I documented an alarming increase in the acquisition of farms, commercial businesses, and production facilities by actors tied to criminal syndicates. On the surface, these transactions looked like simple economic expansion. But beneath them was a calculated strategy to dominate the legitimate economy from within—to fuse legality with criminal enterprise.

My internal reports and threat assessments painted a grim picture: we were facing a silent coup, not by generals, but by gang lords wearing uniforms. The military hierarchy was being hollowed out, repurposed to serve as a protective shell for narco-terrorist operations. Judges, prosecutors, even entire municipal governments were falling—not by gunfire, but by invitation, seduced by money and immunity.

The Delta region became particularly emblematic of this collapse.

With its complex geography, lack of national media attention, and a vulnerable Indigenous population, Delta Amacuro turned into a haven for smuggling, drug trafficking, and non-state armed group expansion. The Orinoco River—once a lifeline of biodiversity—was now a criminal artery connecting gold, cocaine, weapons, and fuel to international markets via Trinidad and Tobago, Guyana, and beyond.

My sources in the field confirmed it: the "Evander Megaband," the Barrancas Syndicate, and the so-called River Pirates had not only displaced Warao communities—they were recruiting from them. Entire ancestral populations were being uprooted or coerced into participating in a war they never chose. The river labyrinths, once sacred territory, had become covert narcotic highways.

By 2019, the death of local warlord Evander Miguel Barradas triggered a power vacuum. His syndicate fragmented, reorganized, and fused with other factions. Some of his lieutenants fled to Trinidad and Tobago to continue operations. Others joined larger criminal networks. Meanwhile, a more dangerous predator emerged—the ELN.

The Colombian guerrilla group, emboldened and expansionist, began advancing deeper into Venezuelan territory. Their confrontation with the Barrancas Syndicate in Barrancas del Orinoco was not just a turf war—it was a battle for control of one of the most strategic drug corridors in the Western Hemisphere. The Orinoco River, cutting across Venezuela and touching Colombia, had become a geopolitical fault line in the new war of hybrid narco-terrorist domination.

On January 1st, armed men wearing red and black armbands opened fire and hurled grenades into the heart of Barrancas during New Year celebrations. The message was clear: the ELN was no longer a guest—it was claiming sovereignty.

Although state forces eventually appeared, the damage had been done. Businesses shuttered. Residents fled. Trust in the government evaporated.

And still, the Cartel de los Soles—the very architects of this systemic breakdown—remained untouched at the highest levels.

The Perfect Storm

Venezuela had become a case study in narco-collapse. Transnational cartels, criminalized military factions, guerrilla insurgents, and economic opportunists now coexisted in a fragile balance of terror. Institutions meant to safeguard the nation were now mechanisms of extortion, repression, or silent complicity.

We were no longer talking about corruption.

We were facing a parallel state.

One that wielded weapons, governed territory, managed cross-border trade—and assassinated those who resisted.

Delta Under Siege

To understand Venezuela's implosion, one must sail into the dense, sacred waters of the Orinoco Delta—a region suspended between the primordial and the profaned. Here, where ancestral canoes once glided in ritual silence, narco-militias now run high-powered boats loaded with cocaine, diesel, scrap metal, weapons, and stolen lives.

The Delta was not just another theatre of collapse. It was the harrowing mirror of a nation's unraveling. A place abandoned by the state, infiltrated by predators, and turned into a lawless convergence point of criminal economies and violent non-state actors.

For years, the region's remoteness—its geographic inaccessibility, its sparse Indigenous population, and near-total media blackout—served as a shield for illicit activity. But that shield shattered when the vacuum left by the death of local warlord Evander Miguel Barradas triggered a brutal reconfiguration of power.

Barradas, head of the Delta Liberation Front (FLD)—also known as the Evander Megaband—had long ruled the Orinoco with calculated terror. His dominion over fuel smuggling, extortion, human trafficking, and drug transit routes made him a feared and indispensable node in Venezuela's criminal economy. His assassination in April 2019 during a supposed confrontation with military and CICPC units was not the end. It was the spark.

What followed was a rapid redistribution of power among fragmented actors: lieutenants who fled to Trinidad and Tobago to continue operations; armed defectors who joined other syndicates; and opportunistic guerrilla factions hungry for dominance. Among them, the Barrancas Syndicate rose as the most notorious and strategically positioned.

Once a movement for labor rights in the state of Monagas, the Barrancas Syndicate morphed into a criminal-political organism, armed and deeply embedded in local institutions. With over a decade of territorial control, hundreds of men under arms, and deep community roots, they were not just tolerated—they were accepted. In some communities, they were seen as the only power that could "resolve conflicts" or "guarantee safety," replacing a vanished state.

But even this formidable structure now faced an external challenger: the National Liberation Army (ELN).

A Criminal River War

The ELN's incursion into Barrancas del Orinoco—the heart of this strategic territory—was no accident. On January 1st, as families gathered to celebrate the New Year, heavily armed men with ELN insignias launched a violent assault on the city. They fired weapons, threw grenades, and left the community in bloodied silence. At least eight people were killed. Dozens fled.

The message was chillingly precise: This is now our territory.

Barrancas del Orinoco's position—where the Orinoco River begins to branch into the Atlantic—makes it a critical hub for smuggling routes. Here, contraband flows to Trinidad and Tobago, chemical inputs for illegal mining arrive, and arms shipments transit undisturbed. It is a geopolitical prize—and the ELN wanted it.

Though they faced resistance from the entrenched Barrancas Syndicate, the ELN had a broader agenda. They were not merely expanding—they were consolidating control of a transnational corridor stretching from the Colombian department of Arauca, through Apure and Bolívar, to Delta Amacuro and the Atlantic Ocean.

Their strategy was textbook insurgent hybrid warfare: infiltrate communities, offer economic alternatives, intimidate rivals, co-opt security forces, and leverage Indigenous knowledge for navigation and concealment.

Collateral Silence: The Warao People

Caught in the crossfire of this criminal chessboard are the Warao people—guardians of the Delta, now displaced, exploited, or co-opted.

Some were forcibly recruited by criminal groups to serve as navigators through the Delta's labyrinthine rivers. Others were pushed off their ancestral lands, fleeing to Brazil, Guyana, or Trinidad and Tobago, where they often fell victim to human trafficking networks. Their stories are absent from national discourse, rendered invisible by a state too compromised—or too complicit—to protect them.

What was once sacred territory is now a logistics platform for warlords.

Reports surfaced of scrap metal dealers collaborating with armed factions to extract materials through Cano Tucupita. River pirates began preying on Indigenous families traveling by boat. Military and police personnel—supposed protectors—were instead described as facilitators, profiting from a cut of every illicit transaction. The state had not only abandoned the Warao. In many cases, it had turned against them.

The Delta as Geopolitical Warning

The Delta Amacuro crisis is not merely a humanitarian disaster. It is a prototype of what happens when a state collapses inward and allows multiple armed groups to contest sovereignty on its soil.

From Barrancas del Orinoco to the remote canals of Tucupita, we are witnessing the birth of a parallel order—one governed by violence, extraction, and criminal diplomacy. Venezuela, once a republic, was fragmenting into a mosaic of occupied zones.

The ELN's expansion is not isolated. It is part of a hemispheric strategy to secure corridors for cocaine, gold, fuel, and weapons. And Venezuela, under the protection of the Cartel de los Soles and the indifference of global institutions, became the most fertile ground imaginable for this insurgent criminal empire.

Barrancas and Arauca share more than geography. They share war economies.

And the river that connects them—the mighty Orinoco—is no longer a symbol of life. It is a contested highway of narco-terrorism.

The Perfect Storm

When criminality becomes governance, and the institutions meant to protect become facilitators of violence, a society crosses an invisible line—one from which it rarely returns. That line was crossed in Venezuela.

What was once sporadic criminal penetration became structural control. What was once denial became normalization. And what was once the exception became the rule.

In Delta Amacuro and the wider eastern corridor of Venezuela, all the critical variables of collapse converged into what I called "The Perfect Storm."

1. A Criminal-State Convergence

The separation between state authority and organized crime dissolved. Governors, judges, high-ranking military officials, and national police commanders were not just turning a blind eye—they were active participants. The Cartel de los Soles, originally an informal network of military officers profiting from drug trafficking, had by then evolved into a full-fledged criminal enterprise embedded in the Venezuelan state.

The Cartel did not operate from the shadows. It wore uniforms. It held press conferences. It led official delegations. Its members sat at the very top of the chain of command, while local operatives controlled everything from airport runways to jungle corridors.

Any remaining line between official duty and criminal profit was obliterated.

2. Fragmented Sovereignty

Multiple criminal factions now competed, cooperated, or coexisted in strategic zones across Venezuela:
   • The ELN (Ejército de Liberación Nacional) operated with strategic precision, controlling mining areas, transit corridors, and rural zones. Their aim was not short-term profit, but sustained territorial control—insurgency disguised as organized crime.

- FARC dissidents, reactivated by the vacuum of power and the retreat of Colombian peace processes, were forging new alliances with Venezuelan syndicates and military officials.
- The Barrancas Syndicate, Tren de Aragua, Los Meleán, and other local factions increasingly merged their operations with regional networks of illegal mining, human trafficking, and cocaine transit.

The result: a Balkanized Venezuela, with zones of parallel authority, shifting alliances, and fluid loyalties. Sovereignty—once centralized—was now leased to the highest bidder.

3. Institutional Paralysis and International Apathy

As the criminal storm escalated, the institutional response disintegrated.

The judiciary became a mechanism of protection for criminal elites. The intelligence apparatus, infiltrated and compromised, became a tool for repression—not investigation. And the military, once a symbol of national sovereignty, now operated with dual agendas: defending the territory while also profiting from its plunder.

International actors—OAS, UNODC, the ICC, and even major powers—chose to look away, distracted by other crises or unwilling to confront the implications of labeling Venezuela what it had become: a narco-terrorist state.

The silence from abroad was not just shameful—it was strategic. It allowed plausible deniability while Venezuelans drowned in a swamp of violence, hunger, and state-sponsored abandonment.

4. Human Collapse: Exodus and Exploitation

Amid this storm, the people were left to fend for themselves—or flee.

The Indigenous Warao, the urban poor, the displaced youth from the interior, and the vulnerable women of riverine communities became both currency and collateral in this new order. Many were coerced into working for the cartels. Others were trafficked or left to perish in silence.

Every institution that once provided a minimal social contract—schools, clinics, police, courts—had become inaccessible, militarized, or defunct.

People no longer asked for justice. They asked only for survival.

5. My Personal Reckoning

As I witnessed this convergence of collapse, infiltration, and despair, I faced a truth I could no longer ignore: the state was lost.

Every operation I led, every seizure, every bust, every strategy was ultimately a partial victory in a war whose command center was already occupied by the enemy. I was not fighting cartels. I was fighting a criminalized regime with the flag of a nation.

And yet—I could not walk away.

To leave the Delta, to abandon the fight, meant to surrender to a future where crime would write the laws, where narco-power would define legitimacy, and where the memory of resistance would be erased by bullets or bureaucracy.

The Perfect Storm was not just geopolitical. It was moral. It was existential.

And it demanded one final act.

Resisting Annihilation

There comes a moment when resistance is not a strategy—but a necessity. A refusal. A line drawn in blood and silence.

Even as threats mounted, allies vanished, and the machinery of the state turned its weapons inward, I made a decision that would define everything that followed:

I would not be silenced.

1. A Final Stand on Shifting Ground

Delta Amacuro was no longer simply a corridor for cocaine. It was a front line in an undeclared war.

The local police, once under my direct operational leadership, were now being pressured by corrupt superiors. The National Guard commanders—many of them with ties to the Cartel de los Soles—began repositioning forces, not to support our operations, but to surveil them. Intelligence I once shared with confidence was now twisted, diluted, or had disappeared.

Yet I pushed forward.

I decentralized my operations. I moved key agents underground. I used encrypted channels to continue communication with trusted allies in the DEA, FBI, and international liaisons. Journalists were given controlled leaks to ensure that our work remained in the public eye. My office became a command post and a sanctuary—until even that began to feel like a trap.

2. They Tried to Erase Me

After the failed assassination attempts and the death of Rodolfo Aurea, I received another coded warning: "They will not miss next time."

And yet—I remained. Not out of recklessness, but conviction.

I knew I had become a symbol, not just to those who wanted me dead, but to those still fighting in silence. Community leaders, young officers, prosecutors in forgotten towns, even military personnel disillusioned by their commanders—all were watching. And I could not allow my disappearance to be just another footnote in Venezuela's catalogue of impunity.

So I spoke louder.

I gave interviews. I sent dossiers to foreign missions. I appeared on regional television to denounce the expansion of cartel operations. I published estimates—based on field intelligence—of cocaine volume leaving the Delta: between 300 and 500 tons annually.

The public began to listen. And so did the enemies.

3. Building a Shadow Alliance

In this hostile terrain, the only way forward was through unconventional solidarity.

I met in secret with officers from the Navy and Air Force—military components still, at that time, less corrupted than the Army and National Guard. I worked with prosecutors disillusioned by the complicity of their superiors. I collaborated with civil society figures, journalists, and members of the Indigenous Warao communities, who risked everything to share intelligence from the jungle corridors.

In essence, I began building a decentralized resistance—not just to drug trafficking, but to the collapse of the Republic.

My vision was not revolutionary. It was restorative.

To bring back the basic principle that justice meant something. That sovereignty wasn't for sale. That no uniform could justify murder.

4. A Cost Paid in Lives

But every step forward costs something.

More agents under my command began receiving threats. Some disappeared. Some, like Rodolfo, were gunned down. Mauro Marcano—brave, vocal, and unflinching—was silenced in the street like a message delivered in blood. Others died in "accidents" too perfectly timed to be a coincidence.

I kept a list. Names I would never forget. A register of resistance paid for in the currency of courage.

And each death made me more certain: this was no longer a fight for law. It was a fight for memory. For dignity. For truth.

5. The Tipping Point

By late 2004, I had reached a singular realization:

The system would not protect me. The system was the threat.

And so I made one final strategic decision: if they were going to take me down, they would have to do it in daylight. Not in silence. Not in a forgotten jungle ambush.

I prepared my final denunciations. I drafted reports naming names—generals, ministers, magistrates. I secured their copies in encrypted formats, delivered them abroad, and prepared a release plan. These were my final insurance policies. Not for me—but for the truth.

If I disappeared, the story would not.

Resisting annihilation was never about survival.

It was about refusing to participate in the death of a nation by remaining silent.

It was about sending a signal to those still fighting: you are not alone.

And it was about holding the line—however fragile, however solitary—between dignity and collapse.

The storm had reached its peak. The enemies were unmasked. The next chapter would be written in exile.

Or not written at all.

Escaping Venezuela

The Final Mission: To Survive

There is a moment when you realize: the war is no longer yours to fight—because the battlefield has become a tomb, and you're the last witness left standing.

1. When the Country Becomes a Cage

The threats no longer came in whispers. They were shouted in the streets, written in slashed tires, painted in the blood of colleagues.

After the death of Mauro Marcano and the murder of my agent Rodolfo Aurea, the message from the Cartel del Sol was unmistakable: "You're next."

Every shadow moved with intention. Every phone call left static and dread. My security protocols became survival rituals. My family was under surveillance. My offices, once hubs of coordinated operations, were now compromised. Friends disappeared, others betrayed me. Even the governor could no longer guarantee protection. There were no more safe places. Only delays.

2. The Last Denunciations

Before I could leave, I had to do one final act: Speak. Loud and clear.

I prepared a last round of classified reports. They named generals, ministers, prosecutors, governors, and foreign intermediaries complicit in the cartel system now absorbing the nation. These documents, encrypted and distributed through trusted international channels, were designed as insurance: if I was killed or captured, the truth would erupt.

I also handed over full copies of field intelligence to the DEA in Caracas, as well as to diplomatic liaisons from Germany, Spain, and the United Kingdom. My final message to them was blunt:

"I can't protect this anymore. But you must not let it vanish."

3. Operation Exodus

The plan to escape had to be silent, fast, and final. Any leak, any hesitation, and I would be dead within hours.

I did not leave as a politician, or even as an intelligence officer.

I left like a hunted man.

There was no official exit. No formal goodbye. I boarded a boat through a clandestine jungle route with only a few allies aware of my departure. From there, by land and air, I navigated a network of safe contacts, moving like contraband across borders.

The jungle, once my operational field, now became my only ally. The river, once patrolled by my teams, became the artery of escape.

It was painful to leave—not out of fear, but because I had not finished the mission. I was abandoning a people, a cause, a battle still raging.

But I knew that if I stayed, I would not live to tell what I had seen. And telling it had become the last act of resistance I could offer.

4. From Witness to Exile

Leaving Tucupita was not a retreat — it was a final maneuver for survival.

My departure was shielded by a friend who is no longer with us: a commissioner from the old DISIP, one of the few loyal men left who still believed in the mission. He organized a discreet caravan to extract me from Delta Amacuro by land, navigating dangerous roads toward the state of Monagas. In Maturín, under deep silence and no trace, I boarded a flight that would take me to a temporary refuge.

That refuge was Trinidad.

There, for several months, I lived in limbo — protected under the discretion of certain authorities, uncertain whether I would ever be able to speak again, or whether my silence would be permanent.

It was in Trinidad where I waited.
Where I watched my homeland from across the sea, burning silently.
Where I processed the war I left behind, and prepared for the war of memory that awaited me.

Eventually, with the coordination and humanitarian support of the Canadian Embassy, I was granted safe passage.
And so I arrived in Canada — not as a traveler, not even as a refugee — but as a bearer of unspeakable testimony.

I did not feel saved.
I felt tasked.

Because now, the responsibility was different. No longer to command teams, or run operations.
Now, the mission was to reconstruct the memory of what had happened.
To warn the world of what had been born in the shadows of Venezuela:

A narco-state with global tentacles.
A prototype of criminal governance that would soon be replicated across continents.

5. The Message They Couldn't Silence

They silenced Mauro.
They killed Rodolfo.
They sent assassins for me.
They tried to erase what we had built.

But they failed.

Because you are reading these words.
Because these pages exist.
Because the truth survived.

From Resistance to Revelation

Exile was not defeat.
    It was resistance transformed.
    The battlefield became the page.
    The bullet became the word.
    And the mission—was reborn.

    This book is not a memoir.
    It is a warning.
    It is evidence.
    It is a torch.

    And the war...
    is not over.

Epilogue – A War That Changed Form

I did not choose exile.
    Exile chose me—as the only remaining trench from which I could keep fighting.

    What I witnessed in Delta Amacuro was not isolated.
    It was not local.
    It was the prototype of a deeper, darker transformation:

    A country collapsing—not by accident, but by design.
    A nation being reconfigured by cartels, corrupt power, and foreign interests.

A model of hybrid criminal governance emerging in plain sight.

I left Venezuela with scars—some visible, others buried.
But what I carried with me was not just memory.
It was evidence, and a profound warning:

That what began in Venezuela would not remain in Venezuela.

The enemy had evolved.
And so must our understanding of war, security, and power.

Toward Chapter 3: The Age of Narco Power

The fall of one country marked the blueprint for many.
In the next chapter, we will dissect how Venezuela became the first modern narco-state—not merely governed by criminals, but restructured by them.
A state where military, politics, and trafficking fused into a single ecosystem of power.

We will uncover:
- The institutional mutation from a republic to a criminal regime.
- The rise of the Cartel of the Suns as a governing body.
- The alliances with Colombian guerrillas, foreign intelligence, and terror groups.
- The exportation of the narco-state model to other parts of Latin America, Africa, and beyond.

What was once an isolated storm became a continental contagion.

And the silence…
is now global.

Chapter 3
THE EMPIRE EXPANDS. From Revolutionary Discourse to a Systemic Narco-State

Governance in Peril

"Behold, you, the leaders who dangle the promise of prosperity before your people, only to ruthlessly betray their trust, plunging headlong into the abyss of corruption and crime. Know this: your shoulders not only carry the crushing burden of your own deeds, but you also sow the insidious seeds of a world spiralling ever deeper into the abyss of corruption, drowning in despair, and teetering on the precipice of Injustice and destruction.". - Johan Obdola

Venezuela's Perilous Decline. The Muscle of the "Cartel de la Revolución"

Strategic Control and Structural Penetration of the State

At the heart of Venezuela's criminal state infrastructure lies a powerful, well-organized, and militarized apparatus that enforces the interests of the regime and facilitates its illicit activities. This structure—referred to internally as the "Cartel de la Revolución"—functions as the muscle of a hybrid criminal-political operation, blurring the boundaries between governance, organized crime, ideological indoctrination, and geopolitical subversion.

Key Figures and Institutions Enabling the Criminal Order:

• **Nicolás Maduro** – President of Venezuela, acting as both symbolic head of state and executive facilitator of the cartel structure.

• **Cilia Flores** – First Lady and powerful political operator with deep influence over the judiciary and intelligence services.

• **Tareck El Aissami** – Former Vice President and architect of the transnational narco-terrorist network; currently detained amidst internal purges.

• General **Néstor Reverol** – Former Minister of Interior and Justice; key figure in National Guard operations and border trafficking corridors.

• **Bolivarian National Guard** – Deployed as a militarized arm of the regime for drug escort, border control, and repression.

• **Venezuelan Army and Air Force** – Complicit in trafficking operations via military bases, clandestine airstrips, and protective convoys.

• **SEBIN (Bolivarian Intelligence Service)** – Functions as a state security apparatus and internal enforcer against dissenters, also instrumental in counter-intelligence and surveillance for the regime.

• **State and Municipal Police Forces** – Controlled directly by the PSUV (United Socialist Party of Venezuela), deployed for coercion, surveillance, and political enforcement.

- **Judicial System** – Including the Supreme Tribunal of Justice and a network of regime-aligned judges, ensures impunity for state-linked criminals and persecution of opposition.

- **Ministry of Public Prosecution** – Politicized and instrumentalized, it obstructs any investigation into state corruption.

- **Governors and Mayors under PSUV** – Local and regional operators, facilitating logistical chains for trafficking and territorial control.

This architecture represents a vertical integration of criminal power, with operatives in uniforms and judges' robes working in tandem with political officials and military command to secure the regime's criminal enterprises. Rather than isolated cases of corruption, what exists in Venezuela is a consolidated criminal governance model, in which state sovereignty has been subverted by cartel logic.

As of 2025, despite internal rivalries and high-profile arrests like that of Tareck El Aissami, the regime continues to maintain strategic coherence through this network, ensuring loyalty through complicity and fear. The interdependence between political power and organized crime is no longer circumstantial—it is foundational.

The Architect of the Hemispheric Narco-Terror Alliance: Tareck El Aissami

Tareck Zaidan El Aissami Maddah, a figure once presented as a technocratic star within the Bolivarian Revolution, has emerged as one of the most dangerous geopolitical actors operating under the protection of a state. His influence extends far beyond Venezuelan borders, embedding itself within a transcontinental network of criminal and terrorist structures linking Latin America, the Middle East, and parts of Europe and Africa.

Born to a Lebanese-Syrian family in El Vigía, Mérida, El Aissami rose rapidly through the political ranks under the tutelage of Hugo Chávez. His early involvement with student movements sympathetic to pan-Arabist and Islamist ideologies marked the beginning of a trajectory that would later transform Venezuela's Ministry of Interior and Justice into an operational hub for transnational criminal entities. As Interior Minister, and later as Vice President, El Aissami oversaw the issuance of Venezuelan identification documents—including passports—to operatives linked to Hezbollah, Hamas, and other extremist groups. U.S. intelligence later confirmed the issuance of at least 173 passports to individuals connected to terrorist networks.

In 2017, the U.S. Department of the Treasury designated El Aissami under the Kingpin Act for playing a significant role in international narcotics trafficking. According to detailed investigations, El Aissami facilitated multiple drug shipments from Venezuela to Mexico and the United States through coordination with notorious Mexican cartels such as Los Zetas and the Sinaloa Cartel. These shipments—often routed through Central America and the Caribbean—were protected by Venezuela's military and intelligence apparatus.

El Aissami's role in supporting Hezbollah's expansion into Latin America is particularly alarming. He has been described by international experts as "the most powerful official of the Venezuelan regime in charge of all the support, financing, and expansion of Hezbollah in the Hemisphere." His ability to broker alliances with Iran's Islamic Revolutionary Guard Corps (IRGC) and Hezbollah operatives—through both state-to-state and covert financial channels—has granted these organizations unprecedented access to the Western Hemisphere.

Among his inner circle is his brother, Feras El Aissami, who reportedly relocated to Uruguay—strategically close to the infamous Tri-Border Area (TBA) between Argentina, Brazil, and Paraguay. This zone has long served as a safe haven for terrorist financing, weapons smuggling, and money laundering. Multiple reports have placed Hezbollah-linked operatives in this area, generating upwards of $43 billion annually through drug trafficking, weapons sales, and human trafficking operations.

Further complicating the geopolitical landscape is the presence of Ghazi Nasr Al-Din, a Lebanese-born Venezuelan diplomat wanted by the FBI. Al-Din allegedly facilitated Hezbollah fundraising activities and helped establish a Hezbollah-linked cultural center in Venezuela. According to FBI and DEA reports, Al-Din frequently traveled between Caracas and Beirut, coordinating both political cover and operational logistics for terrorist elements.

These actors have not operated in isolation. Their activities have been protected, financed, and legitimized by the highest levels of the Venezuelan government. The collaboration between criminal networks, ideological extremists, and state officials has created a hybrid narco-terrorist ecosystem—one that threatens not only Venezuelan sovereignty but also regional and international stability.

El Aissami's strategic positioning in key ministries allowed him to become a central broker in this web of illicit relations. Even after being reassigned as Minister of Industries and National Production in 2018, his influence over the military, intelligence services, and logistical corridors of illicit trade remained unchallenged. His removal in 2023 amid corruption investigations was less a repudiation of his activities than a tactical repositioning within the regime's internal power dynamics.

The case of Tareck El Aissami illustrates how Venezuela's collapse into criminality has not been incidental or chaotic, but deliberate and engineered. El Aissami did not merely exploit a broken system—he helped design and operationalize it. His trajectory epitomizes the dangerous fusion of political power, ideological radicalism, and organized crime, marking him as one of the architects of the Hemispheric Narco-Terror Alliance.

The Hezbollah Connection – Venezuela's Strategic Bridge to Transnational Terrorism

Strategic Convergence and the Expansion of Proxy Networks

The entanglement of the Venezuelan regime with Hezbollah represents one of the most alarming and underreported elements of the country's transformation into a narco-terrorist state. This strategic alliance, forged during the Chávez-Ahmadinejad era and deepened under Maduro, reflects not only geopolitical defiance toward the West but the deliberate integration of Venezuela into a global web of extremist financing, ideological propagation, and paramilitary logistics.

Tareck El Aissami, long known for his ties to Hezbollah and Iran, played a pivotal role in building the operational architecture that allowed Hezbollah to establish financial and logistical hubs across Latin America. As noted in prior intelligence assessments, Aissami's brother, Feras El Aissami, relocated to Uruguay, bringing Hezbollah's interests closer to the Tri-Border Area (TBA)—a hotbed for illicit financial transactions and narcotics trade among Argentina, Brazil, and Paraguay.

The FBI's open investigations into figures like Ghazi Nasr Al-Din—another Hezbollah-linked operative naturalized in Venezuela—further illustrate how the Maduro regime has empowered a foreign terrorist network to operate with diplomatic cover and immunity. Al-Din, once a diplomat at the Venezuelan Embassy in Syria, allegedly facilitated donations and logistics for Hezbollah, even launching a Hezbollah-aligned community center in Venezuela.

Hezbollah's Economic and Operational Footprint

According to security analysts and U.S. officials, Hezbollah now earns over $1.1 billion USD annually, much of it through narcotics, arms, and human trafficking—some of which is directly connected to Venezuelan territory. Reports from U.S. Southern Command and the State Department confirm that operatives have been stationed in countries like Bolivia and Peru, using Venezuelan IDs and financial infrastructure to coordinate operations. In the TBA, Hezbollah and other groups allegedly channel over $43 billion annually from illicit enterprises.

Former counterterrorism expert Johan Obdola highlights how Hezbollah's presence in Latin America has evolved from passive funding to active involvement in drug corridors, logistical operations, and influence campaigns. "The Venezuelan regime has been providing assistance to Hezbollah since 2005," Obdola noted. "It began with facilitating documentation and passports, but quickly evolved into allowing operatives to freely travel and establish networks across Central and South America."

Iran's Ideological and Cultural Offensive: A Hybrid Warfare Strategy

The strategic cooperation between Iran and Venezuela is not limited to covert financial and logistical support. The cultural and ideological front has become a new battlefield. One symbolic example is the state-sponsored distribution of the book "Mi Tío Soleimani"

("My Uncle Soleimani") in Venezuelan schools, targeting youth with radicalized narratives glorifying martyrdom and anti-Western ideology. This initiative, coordinated by the Iranian Embassy and Caracas officials, represents a calculated soft power strategy—a fusion of indoctrination, soft colonization, and psychological warfare.

Through its network of cultural centers, Iran promotes Shi'a ideology under the guise of diplomacy, while Cuba provides technical expertise in social control. This "axis of influence" uses Venezuela as a geopolitical beachhead to shape the region's ideological alignment and destabilize pro-democratic governments.

Implications and Emerging Threat Vectors

The fusion of criminal governance and ideological extremism positions Venezuela as an unprecedented hybrid threat in the Western Hemisphere. The Hezbollah-Venezuela alliance is no longer just a political scandal—it is an evolving security challenge for the Americas. This strategic marriage of convenience gives Iran and Hezbollah direct access to U.S. borders, maritime routes, and strategic resources through a criminalized state apparatus.

As such, dismantling these networks will require far more than sanctions or isolated arrests. It will demand a transnational strategy based on intelligence-sharing, regional coordination, and the political will to confront a state actor that no longer functions within the confines of international norms.

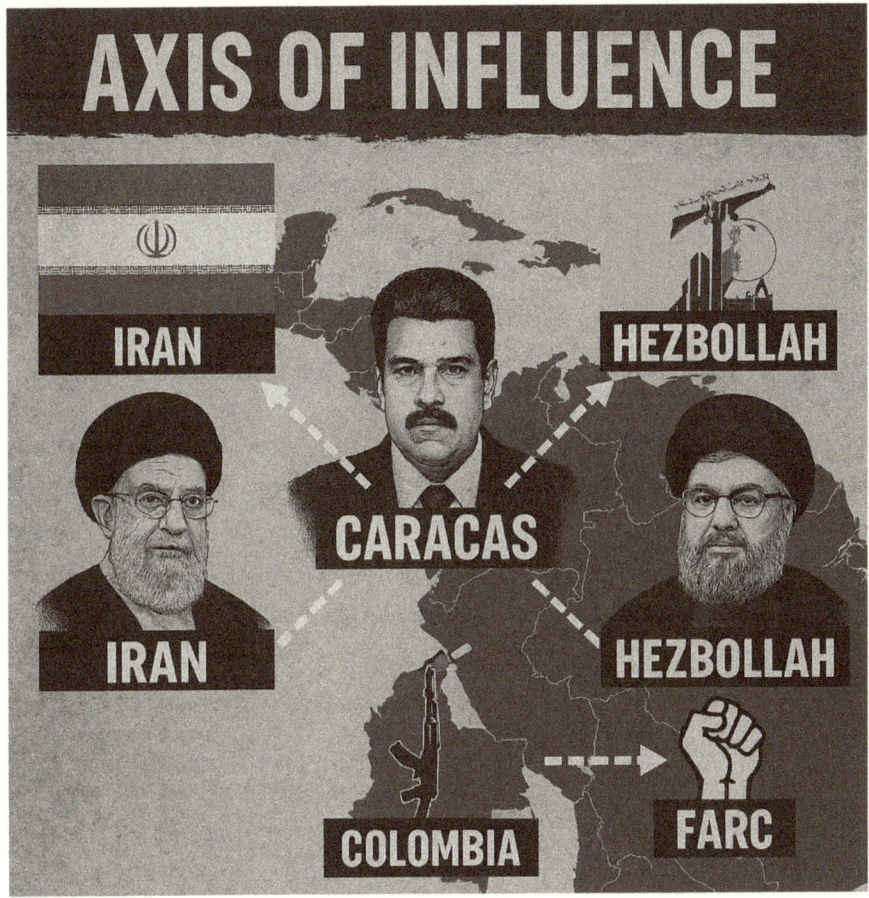

The Cocaine Revolution — From Chávez to Maduro: Terror, Trafficking, and State Capture

The Rise of a Narcotic Empire

What began as a concealed alignment between the Bolivarian regime and narcotrafficking factions under Hugo Chávez has evolved into a fully operational narco-terrorist state. This transformation is not a matter of mere speculation—it is a structural reality rooted in decades of institutional decay, strategic criminal collusion, and state-sanctioned impunity.

The so-called Cocaine Revolution—a term that may once have sounded alarmist—now defines the very architecture of Venezuela's economy and governance. With oil revenues collapsing and traditional sources of national income eroded, the Chávez-Maduro regime turned increasingly to illicit economies to maintain political control. Drug trafficking became not only an economic instrument but a tool of geopolitical leverage, foreign influence, and domestic repression.

Institutional Complicity: The Role of PDVSA and the Military

The state-owned oil company PDVSA has become one of the regime's principal vehicles for money laundering and international criminal transactions. Once the pride of Venezuela's industrial prowess, PDVSA has degenerated into a dark financial artery—used to channel illicit funds, enable transnational trafficking routes, and support proxy operations in Africa, Europe, and the Middle East.

Parallel to this, Venezuela's military apparatus—particularly elite factions of the Bolivarian National Armed Forces (FANB)—has been transformed into a protective shield for the cocaine trade. Military airstrips have been co-opted, border checkpoints neutralized, and naval operations corrupted. Intelligence reports and testimonies confirm that certain units are directly involved in protecting and facilitating drug routes, especially those connecting Apure, Zulia, and Amazonas to Colombia, the Caribbean, and West Africa.

The PSUV and the Cocaine State

The ruling party, Partido Socialista Unido de Venezuela (PSUV), has fully embedded itself within this illicit framework. What was once a political movement born from a populist revolution has mutated into a criminal syndicate that funds its electoral campaigns through narco-dollars. The proceeds of cocaine, gold smuggling, and illicit financial flows are used to finance repression, secure loyalty through patronage networks, and manipulate the country's electoral and judicial institutions.

This hybridization of political power and criminal enterprise has hollowed out what remains of Venezuela's democratic structures. It is not just a failed state—it is a captured one.

The Shadow of Diosdado Cabello: A Cartel within the State

Among the most emblematic figures in Venezuela's transformation into a narco-state stands Diosdado Cabello, widely regarded by U.S. intelligence agencies as the operational head of the Cartel de los Soles. This cartel—named after the golden insignias of Venezuelan military officers—originated as a network of corrupt generals and has since expanded into a regional empire with tentacles in human trafficking, illegal mining, arms trading, and cocaine production.

U.S. federal indictments and intelligence reports have identified Cabello not just as an enabler but as the mastermind behind much of the regime's criminal architecture. His proximity to state institutions grants him access to logistics, protection, and global networks, including those connected to Hezbollah, the Sinaloa Cartel, and FARC dissidents.

Evidence and Consequences

The U.S. Justice Department, Treasury, DEA, and FinCEN have sanctioned and indicted hundreds of individuals and entities linked to the Venezuelan regime. Despite these efforts, the sheer scale of criminal penetration into every layer of government makes dismantling the narco-state a near-impossible task without regional and multilateral coordination.

The fallout is catastrophic:
- Entire regions of Venezuela are now effectively governed by criminal groups.
- Border towns and states have become hubs for trafficking, violence, and arms proliferation.
- The state's failure to control its territory has invited paramilitary forces, guerrillas, and foreign operatives to fill the void.

What was once a nation of immense promise is now a geopolitical epicenter of criminal convergence—a threat that reaches beyond its borders into Colombia, the Caribbean, Central America, and even Europe.

Closing Insight: The Criminalization of Sovereignty

The Cocaine Revolution has led to the criminalization of the Venezuelan state itself. The institutions meant to safeguard the nation's sovereignty have instead weaponized that sovereignty to protect criminal activities from international accountability. The regime's survival depends not on popular legitimacy or economic production but on its capacity to navigate and manipulate global illicit markets.

This is not simply a crisis of governance—it is a crisis of civilization.

The Shadow Alliance — Venezuela, Hezbollah, and the Geopolitics of Terror

Convergence of Agendas: When Narco-State Meets Proxy Warfare

Beyond drug trafficking and systemic corruption, the Maduro regime has embraced a far more dangerous dimension of international criminal alignment: the integration of state-sponsored terrorism into its foreign and domestic doctrine.

This convergence has manifested through Venezuela's increasingly strategic relationship with Iran, Hezbollah, and other extremist proxies. It is a geopolitical arrangement rooted not in ideology, but in mutual interest: protection, money laundering, illicit logistics, and regional destabilization. Together, they form what can only be described as a "shadow alliance"—a convergence of narcotics, terrorism, and authoritarian statecraft.

Hezbollah's Presence in Latin America

For over two decades, Hezbollah has established operational cells across Latin America, using Venezuela as a critical base of operations. These activities include:
• Money laundering via currency exchange houses and front businesses in Caracas, Maracaibo, and Margarita Island.
• Identity falsification and passport networks, as revealed by investigations into the Venezuelan Ministry of Interior and the SAIME identity agency.
• Drug trafficking and weapons procurement, often in coordination with local criminal gangs and state-protected air corridors.

The Tri-Border Area (TBA) between Paraguay, Brazil, and Argentina has long been a logistical sanctuary for Hezbollah operatives, but Venezuela has provided something even more dangerous: state protection.

This alliance is not incidental. It is designed, nurtured, and funded.

The Iran-Venezuela Strategic Nexus

Iran, under the leadership of Ayatollah Khamenei and with operational arms like the IRGC and Quds Force, has found in Venezuela both an ideological ally and a geopolitical beachhead in the Western Hemisphere.

Some of the key developments include:
• Dozens of cultural centers and schools promoting Shiite ideology and anti-Western narratives.
• Oil-for-technology exchanges, including the shipment of fuel, refinery parts, and even surveillance systems.
• Military cooperation, with reports of IRGC-linked trainers providing instruction to Venezuelan special forces and intelligence agents.

In return, Venezuela grants Iran access to gold, uranium, and strategic influence over regional anti-U.S. agendas.

The alliance is deeply entrenched in symbolism, as evidenced by public tributes to Qasem Soleimani and official events that glorify Iranian martyrs within Caracas. These acts are not mere gestures—they signal Venezuela's ideological alignment with anti-democratic, theocratic governance models.

Cultural Indoctrination as Strategy

The presentation of the children's book "My Uncle Soleimani" in Caracas—attended by the Iranian ambassador and top regime officials—was more than propaganda. It was indoctrination.

Distributed across Venezuela, Ecuador, and Colombia, this publication attempts to reframe Soleimani as a heroic figure to Latin American youth. It is part of a long-term strategy to embed Iranian revolutionary mythology within the social fabric of a collapsing Venezuelan state.

Furthermore, the creation of the children's magazine "Primer Paso", presented as an educational tool, embeds soft-power influence and opens new terrain for ideological recruitment. These publications serve the dual purpose of cultural colonization and emotional manipulation in an already vulnerable society.

Terror Routes and Global Risk

The convergence of Venezuela's narco-state with Iran's proxy networks has transformed the country into:
- A logistical bridge for money, drugs, and weapons.
- A diplomatic shield for wanted operatives.
- A financial hub for evading sanctions through cryptocurrency, gold, and informal networks.

This hybrid alliance undermines not only regional democracies but global counterterrorism efforts. Hezbollah's access to Venezuelan territory, ports, and airspace enables operations with transatlantic reach—including into Europe and West Africa.

As highlighted by U.S. Southern Command and European intelligence briefings, the presence of these groups poses a direct threat to NATO countries, as well as to partners in the Americas.

Geopolitical Implications: The Axis Expands

This shadow alliance cannot be seen in isolation. It is part of a broader "Axis of Influence" involving:
- Venezuela (Narco-state and logistics center)
- Iran (Ideological architect and logistical partner)
- Russia (Cyber, intelligence, and political support)
- Cuba (Counterintelligence and ideological training)
- China (Financial leverage and surveillance systems)

Together, these actors coordinate across multiple domains: propaganda, economic penetration, social control, and asymmetric warfare.

Conclusion: A Red Flag for the Western Hemisphere

The alliance between Venezuela and Iran, and by extension Hezbollah, is not a side effect of instability—it is a strategic arrangement. Through cultural indoctrination, state protection of terrorist groups, and the instrumentalization of public institutions, the Maduro regime has transformed Venezuela into a conduit of terrorism in the Americas.

The New Doctrine — The Cartel of the Suns and the Militarization of Crime

Origins of the Cartel of the Suns (Cartel de los Soles)

The Cartel de los Soles—so named for the golden sun insignias worn by Venezuelan generals—emerged not as a rogue faction, but as a parallel structure of state power embedded within the Bolivarian Revolution. What began as isolated involvement of military officials in drug trafficking operations has since evolved into one of the most sophisticated narco-military networks in the Western Hemisphere.

Rooted within the Venezuelan armed forces (FANB), this cartel operates under the protection of the state, with direct access to logistical routes, intelligence infrastructure, diplomatic immunity, and financial systems. It is not a criminal enterprise infiltrating the state—it is the state.

Structure and Key Actors

The organizational structure of the Cartel de los Soles is tiered and militarized. Its command structure includes:

- **Top-Level Commanders:** High-ranking generals and political officials, including those in the Ministries of Defense and Interior.
- **Mid-Level Operatives:** Military officers overseeing airports, border posts, and maritime routes. Many of these individuals serve as regional "plaza bosses."
- **Operational Fronts:** Logistics coordinators managing airstrips, cargo routes, and informal financial circuits. These often involve PDVSA officials and customs agents.

Among the most prominent figures identified by U.S. authorities and international investigations are:

- **Diosdado Cabello:** Former military officer and one of the most powerful political figures in Venezuela. Alleged mastermind and protector of the cartel's interests.

- **Néstor Reverol:** Former Minister of Interior and Justice, sanctioned for direct involvement in drug trafficking and cover-up operations.
- **Hugo Carvajal ("El Pollo"):** Former intelligence chief, extradited to the U.S. in 2022 on charges of narcotics conspiracy and arms trafficking.
- **Clíver Alcalá Cordones:** Retired general who eventually surrendered to U.S. authorities and became a cooperating witness.

The cartel's power lies not only in its access, but in its institutional legitimacy. It commands uniforms, controls borders, and navigates within the protections of sovereignty.

Modus Operandi: From Jungle to Global Markets

The cartel's operational footprint spans multiple continents. Key components of its modus operandi include:

- **Air Bridges:** Use of clandestine airstrips in Apure, Zulia, and Amazonas to launch drug flights to Honduras, Mexico, and West Africa.
- **Naval Routes:** Deployment of semi-submersibles and disguised fishing vessels along Venezuela's Caribbean coast.
- **Border Corridors:** Control of smuggling routes through Táchira and Bolívar, often in collaboration or conflict with ELN and FARC dissidents.
- **Diplomatic Channels:** Use of embassies, diplomatic pouches, and state-owned companies for laundering and trafficking.

Through these routes, cocaine sourced from Colombia is processed, packaged, and shipped under the supervision—or direct participation—of military and intelligence officials.

The Fusion of Doctrine and Crime

What makes the Cartel de los Soles particularly dangerous is its ideological camouflage. Framed within the Bolivarian doctrine of anti-imperialism and revolutionary defense, it justifies its operations as part of a "resistance economy." This narrative is used to:

- Delegitimize international investigations and sanctions.
- Mobilize domestic political support.
- Integrate criminal actors into governance through party structures.

This is not merely a criminal operation—it is a doctrinal weaponization of crime, used to fund political survival and geopolitical defiance.

Militarization of Corruption: The State as a Hybrid Actor

Unlike traditional cartels, the Cartel de los Soles does not fear the state—it is protected by it. This represents a shift in how we understand organized crime. Venezuela is not a failed state—it is a repurposed state, engineered to sustain illicit activity as an instrument of governance.

Key indicators of this hybrid model include:
- Legal immunity for implicated officials.
- Rotation of sanctioned individuals into diplomatic or party roles.
- Use of national intelligence services (SEBIN, DGCIM) to neutralize internal dissent.

This model blurs the lines between national defense, political propaganda, and transnational crime.

International Response and the Intelligence Gap

Despite years of evidence and indictments, the Cartel de los Soles remains operational, in part due to:
- Weak multilateral enforcement mechanisms.
- Fear of confrontation with a sovereign regime.
- Inconsistent coordination between Western intelligence agencies.

However, momentum has been building. U.S. agencies have levied multiple indictments, and the DEA has identified Venezuela as a primary hub in the global cocaine trade. The European Union, meanwhile, has expanded sanctions and prohibited military exports. But strategic action remains fragmented.

There is an urgent need for:
- A transnational criminal designation of the Venezuelan regime.
- Unified intelligence-sharing frameworks.
- Financial interdiction systems to target military-linked enterprises.

Conclusion: Venezuela as a Case Study of State-Crime Integration

The Cartel de los Soles is not merely a criminal organization—it is the definitive proof that Venezuela has become a narco-militarized state, where doctrine, power, and profit converge.

The implications are vast: regional destabilization, emboldened criminal syndicates, human rights abuses, and a redefinition of state legitimacy itself.

Venezuela's transformation must serve as a case study for global institutions: a warning that criminal networks no longer need to infiltrate states when they can simply become the state.

Collapse by Design — PDVSA, Human Trafficking, and the Economics of Chaos

The Engineered Implosion of a National Symbol

Once the pride of Venezuela and the financial backbone of Latin America's energy sector, PDVSA (Petróleos de Venezuela S.A.) has been hollowed out—repurposed from a national oil company into a multinational criminal apparatus. Its collapse was not incidental, nor merely the result of mismanagement. It was strategically orchestrated, transforming PDVSA into a mechanism for money laundering, trafficking, and elite enrichment.

As oil output plummeted from nearly 3.5 million barrels per day in the late 1990s to under 700,000 by 2023, the company became a shell for parallel operations: gold smuggling, human trafficking, arms exchanges, and offshore banking.

This process aligned with a broader criminalization of the state economy, where the line between public enterprise and private mafia was erased.

The Triple Nexus: Oil, Corruption, and Illicit Flows

PDVSA became the epicenter of Venezuela's illicit financial system through three core vectors:

1. Laundering of Oil Revenues: Artificially inflated contracts, ghost companies, and opaque pricing structures allowed billions of dollars to be siphoned to offshore accounts and luxury assets.

2. Gold-for-Oil Exchanges: In coordination with groups like Hezbollah, ELN, and Iranian proxies, PDVSA facilitated covert trade networks involving gold, fuel, and weapons. Maracaibo and Bolívar became strategic nodes in this chain.

3. Human Trafficking Corridors: Under the guise of logistical operations, PDVSA vehicles, maritime routes, and infrastructure were used to traffic migrants, women, and minors, often with the complicity of military and security forces.

This criminal conversion of Venezuela's most strategic asset became the economic pillar of the narco-regime.

Trafficking in Flesh and Shadows

Venezuela's descent into chaos has created fertile ground for human trafficking networks. The collapse of legal systems, economic desperation, and porous borders have made the country both an origin and transit point for:

• Sexual exploitation rings—particularly targeting women and girls in rural areas, transported to mining regions or exported to the Caribbean and Europe.

• Forced labor routes—often involving Indigenous populations coerced into mining, coca cultivation, or illegal logging.

• Child recruitment pipelines—linked to FARC dissidents, ELN, and even Middle Eastern groups operating through Venezuela's intelligence networks.

The criminal economy thrives on institutional passivity and deliberate facilitation. Shell companies, proxy businesses, and diplomatic cover have been used to conceal assets and movements.

A 2022 U.S. State Department report confirmed that senior regime-linked individuals used transnational entities to store and move wealth, often overlapping with trafficking operations.

The Economics of Criminal Sovereignty

What we are witnessing is not just kleptocracy—it is a form of criminal sovereignty, where the state sustains itself not through taxes or productivity, but through illicit economies.

Under Maduro, Venezuela's shadow economy now accounts for an estimated 30–40% of GDP, according to intelligence assessments and independent economic monitors. This includes:

• Narcotics production and transit fees
• Illicit mining and gold exports
• Extortion "taxes" by paramilitary groups
• Human smuggling and migrant exploitation

The regime no longer pretends to pursue recovery—it has re-engineered collapse as governance.

International Response and the Limits of Enforcement

In response, the United States and European allies have escalated enforcement efforts:
- FinCEN advisories issued against Venezuelan banking institutions.
- Over 300 individuals and entities sanctioned under OFAC, including PDVSA executives, military officials, and family networks.
- DOJ indictments and asset freezes on more than $2 billion in overseas holdings.

Yet, the regime's transnational laundering architecture remains adaptive, often migrating operations to jurisdictions with weaker enforcement capacity.

Meanwhile, the collapse of PDVSA has regional ripple effects: energy instability in the Caribbean, smuggling across Colombia and Brazil, and increased migration flows overwhelming border nations.

Conclusion: The State as a Trafficker

Venezuela's ruling elite has redefined the concept of state enterprise—not as a provider of goods and services, but as a logistical cover for transnational crime.

PDVSA is no longer a company. It is a criminal consortium, embedded within a government that profits from despair, erases accountability, and thrives in chaos.

The country's collapse is not a failure to govern—it is the chosen mode of governance.

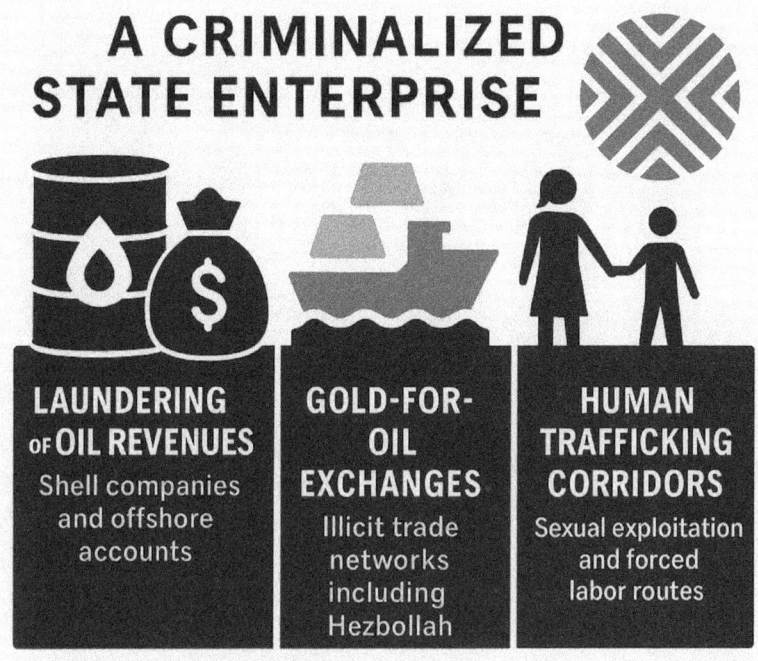

- 30-40% of GDP estimated to be shadow economy
- Collapse of company used as logistical cover for transnational crime
- Senior officials implicated in operations

PDVSA: The Engine of a Criminal Economy

1. PDVSA's Fall from National Pride to Criminal Enterprise

Once the cornerstone of Venezuela's economy and a source of national pride, Petróleos de Venezuela S.A. (PDVSA) has descended into the heart of a complex criminal ecosystem. Once among the top five oil producers globally, PDVSA now serves as a central vehicle for laundering money, facilitating illegal financial operations, and supporting transnational crime. Under Chávez, and even more aggressively under Maduro, PDVSA became not just a tool of state policy but a parallel criminal economy.

As production collapsed—from over 3.2 million barrels per day in 1998 to under 700,000 in recent years—PDVSA was repurposed. The institution was militarized, politicized, and systematically hollowed out, becoming a nucleus for illicit enrichment by the elite. Oil shipments were rerouted through opaque contracts to favored partners, often under the guise of political solidarity with allies such as Iran, Cuba, and China.

2. Oil-for-Drugs, Oil-for-Criminal Loyalty

PDVSA has been at the core of a sophisticated "oil-for-criminal-loyalty" mechanism. Oil, often sold at steep discounts or bartered for illicit goods and services, became a currency in itself. Intelligence reports and independent investigations have revealed that crude oil shipments were used to finance not only political allies abroad but criminal partners at home.

Some shipments were diverted entirely to the black market; others ended up exchanged for weapons, narcotics, and cash. This strategy ensured continued loyalty from key military units, foreign cartels, and radicalized groups operating under Venezuela's shadow influence.

3. Internal Criminal Networks and Foreign Penetration

Inside PDVSA, multiple criminal networks operated simultaneously. The "Red de Enriquecimiento Petrolero" (Oil Enrichment Network) tied together directors, security forces, and intermediaries managing fake service contracts, inflated invoices, and phantom shipments. Billions were funneled out of Venezuela through fake consultancies, offshore accounts, and illicit gold exchanges.

In parallel, foreign actors—particularly from Iran, Russia, and Turkey—penetrated PDVSA's finance and logistics structures. These governments used PDVSA not only as an economic opportunity but as a political instrument to challenge U.S. sanctions and support rogue actors worldwide.

4. Gold, Sex, and Fuel: The PDVSA Crime Triangle

PDVSA's facilities and operational arms also became hubs for human and sexual trafficking. Intelligence sources have confirmed that fuel smuggling routes were used to transport women and children, often from the interior states of Venezuela, into international criminal circuits. In return, illicit actors provided luxury goods, hard currency, and protection.

The intersections of illicit gold, fuel, and sex trafficking became an unofficial economic model in the collapsed oil towns of Zulia, Bolívar, and Anzoátegui—regions now effectively under narco-militarized governance.

5. Financial Forensics and International Indictments

The U.S. Treasury Department, along with FinCEN and the Department of Justice, has tracked PDVSA-related laundering schemes through multiple jurisdictions: Panama, the Caribbean, Spain, and Eastern Europe. Over 300 individuals and companies have been sanctioned or indicted in connection with PDVSA corruption. However, many remain protected under Venezuelan immunity agreements and foreign intelligence pacts.

Among those charged are close relatives of key PSUV figures, senior PDVSA administrators, and even supposed "technocrats" installed during recent management purges meant to feign reform.

6. Collapse and Conversion: PDVSA as Narco-State Nexus

In its current form, PDVSA no longer functions as a traditional energy corporation. It is now a hybrid narco-financial apparatus with embedded loyalties to non-state actors, criminal networks, and foreign regimes. Its infrastructure has been converted into a platform for laundering, trafficking, and destabilization, with limited oversight and maximum impunity.

PDVSA has become the ultimate symbol of Venezuela's transition from a state-led development model to a full-blown criminal state—where oil is no longer for the people, but for the preservation of a narco-terrorist regime.

The Foreign Web: Iran, Hezbollah, and the Geopolitical Nexus

1. The Strategic Alliance Between Caracas and Tehran

The Maduro regime's alliance with the Islamic Republic of Iran represents a deep geopolitical realignment, one that transcends economics and ideology. It is a convergence rooted in mutual hostility toward the United States, a shared commitment to authoritarian resilience, and a tactical use of asymmetric warfare tools.

Iran, through its Islamic Revolutionary Guard Corps (IRGC), has viewed Venezuela as a forward-operating platform in the Western Hemisphere. In exchange for political loyalty and territorial access, Iran has provided Maduro's regime with military equipment, surveillance technologies, refinery support, and a highly sophisticated network of financial and diplomatic backing.

2. Hezbollah's Embedding and Operational Footprint

Hezbollah, the Lebanese-based proxy of the IRGC, has capitalized on this alliance to entrench itself across Latin America—most notably in Venezuela, Colombia, and the Tri-Border Area. In Venezuela, the organization has enjoyed privileged status, operating under diplomatic cover, controlling cargo shipments, laundering through front companies, and facilitating arms and narcotics logistics in coordination with local military and intelligence units.

Multiple intelligence assessments—confirmed by U.S. Southern Command and regional agencies—indicate that Hezbollah operatives have received Venezuelan documentation, participated in gold and diamond smuggling routes, and played a crucial role in training pro-regime militias.

3. The Cultural Front: Iranian Indoctrination Centers in Venezuela

Parallel to its military and intelligence operations, Iran has established a growing number of "cultural centers" across Venezuela—especially in Caracas, Valencia, Maracay, and Barinas. Under the guise of educational and religious exchange, these institutions have become soft power outposts for Shi'a fundamentalist indoctrination.

Events such as the publication of *My Uncle Soleimani* and the children's magazine *Primer Paso*—presented with Venezuelan officials at Plaza Bolívar—reflect a long-term strategy: implant ideological loyalty to Iran's revolutionary values among Venezuela's youth. These centers are also used to monitor dissidents, build community surveillance networks, and propagate an anti-Western narrative deeply aligned with Tehran's worldview.

4. Financial Synergies: The Black Money Network

Iran and Venezuela have developed a mutual mechanism for bypassing sanctions, using complex barter systems, cryptocurrency wallets, and gold smuggling to maintain liquidity. Oil-for-gold transactions have been facilitated via opaque transport routes through Turkey and the Caribbean. Cryptocurrency mining farms, protected by Venezuelan military intelligence (DGCIM), have been linked to Iranian interests, as has the illicit sale of industrial materials extracted from the Orinoco region.

Hezbollah operatives have been active in managing these networks, converting cash into stable assets, and moving funds through European and Middle Eastern shell entities. The overlap between PDVSA, Hezbollah's logistics, and Iranian intelligence marks Venezuela as one of the most active narco-financial theaters in the world.

5. The Military Intelligence Convergence

DGCIM and SEBIN, Venezuela's main intelligence agencies, have adopted Iranian methodologies for domestic surveillance, dissent control, and cyber-monitoring. Iranian advisors—some of them ex-IRGC—have been embedded within these institutions since at least 2017. They have helped establish espionage centers, disrupt opposition movements, and train "technological brigades" for population monitoring.

This alignment of intelligence doctrines forms part of a broader strategy of regime survival through repression, deterrence, and hybrid warfare. It also reinforces Maduro's international legitimacy among autocratic partners such as Syria, North Korea, and Russia.

6. Implications for Hemispheric Security

This foreign web—anchored by Iran and Hezbollah—presents a unique and enduring threat to hemispheric security. Venezuela is no longer a failed state; it is a purposefully restructured platform for global destabilization. Its integration with Islamic fundamentalist networks, state-sponsored terrorism, and transnational criminal structures puts Latin America on the frontline of a new form of hybrid geopolitical warfare.

From ideological penetration of youth to intelligence collaboration and narco-financial flows, this alliance positions Venezuela as both an exporter of chaos and a test case for the convergence of narco-terrorism and authoritarian diplomacy.

Institutional Decomposition and the Expansion of Transnational Criminal Networks

The Collapse of Rule of Law and the Rise of the Criminal Ecosystem

The Venezuelan state today exhibits the characteristics of what security analysts define as a "criminalized hybrid regime"—a government that retains the external appearance of sovereignty but internally operates as a facilitator of transnational criminal enterprise.

Over the past two decades, the systematic weakening of democratic institutions, combined with the militarization of civilian governance, has opened unprecedented space for criminal networks to flourish. Venezuelan law enforcement, customs, immigration, and judicial sectors have become either infiltrated or co-opted by criminal and political actors with direct links to narcotrafficking organizations, money laundering cells, arms brokers, and terrorist facilitators.

At the center of this collapse lies the erosion of the rule of law. Public institutions no longer serve the common good or uphold legal accountability. Instead, they operate as instruments of political repression and facilitators of illicit economies. The judiciary has lost autonomy. Anti-corruption bodies exist in name only. Investigative journalism is criminalized. Civil society actors face intimidation, exile, or imprisonment.

The consequence is a functional convergence between criminal networks and state structures. Organized crime groups no longer operate in the shadows—they operate with impunity under the protection or collaboration of state entities. The blurred lines between political power and criminal enterprise have produced what some scholars now refer to as a "Post-Sovereign Criminal State"—a regime where the state is no longer a deterrent to organized crime, but a host and engine for its expansion.

The Venezuelan military and intelligence services have played a decisive role in this convergence. Units such as the General Directorate of Military Counterintelligence (DGCIM) and the Bolivarian National Intelligence Service (SEBIN) have been repeatedly implicated in activities ranging from drug protection to the persecution of internal dissenters. These entities, rather than serving national security, function today as elite protection corps for the regime and its criminal allies.

Furthermore, Venezuela's ungoverned territories—including large swaths of the Amazon, the Orinoco mining belt, and the Colombian border—have become zones of criminal sovereignty, controlled not by the state, but by guerrilla groups, syndicates, and foreign actors like Hezbollah and the FARC/Dissidents. These areas serve as trafficking corridors, illegal mining enclaves, and operational sanctuaries for armed groups with hemispheric ambitions.

Key Insight Box

Venezuela's State Transformation Model
- From: State-as-Sovereign Actor
- To: State-as-Criminal Hub
- Characteristics:
- Politicized judiciary and silenced media
- Security forces as protectors of illicit networks
- Territorial fragmentation and guerrilla presence

- Export of corruption as foreign policy tool
- Weak or absent regulatory institutions

Transition To Section 9

The unraveling of Venezuela's institutional integrity has not only affected domestic governance—it has redefined the country's geopolitical alignments and external alliances. In the next section, we will explore how Venezuela has forged and exploited relationships with rogue states and non-state actors to entrench its criminal governance model and circumvent hemispheric isolation.

Strategic Convergence: Cartels, Theocracies, and State Capture

When Crime Becomes Policy, and Policy Becomes Crime

In the twenty-first century, Venezuela has become the archetype of a hybrid narco-theocratic state — one where the lines between ideology, criminal economy, and geopolitical maneuvering have fully converged. What began under Chávez as a revolutionary banner against "imperialism" evolved into a complex architecture of illicit alliances, institutional corruption, and militant entanglements with Iran, Hezbollah, FARC, and transregional cartels.

By 2024, the Venezuelan regime had effectively embedded this structure into national governance. Ministries, military commands, and diplomatic outposts no longer served public interests but instead functioned as operational nodes in a vast illicit economy. From the Tri-Border Area in South America to Lebanese enclaves and Middle Eastern cultural centers, the Venezuelan state had become a platform for proxy warfare, smuggling logistics, terror financing, and hybrid influence operations.

This strategic convergence did not occur spontaneously. It was carefully orchestrated through a progressive capture of institutions:

- The Military was transformed into a profit-driven structure tied to cocaine production, arms trafficking, and gold mining.
- PDVSA, once a symbol of national wealth, became a shell corporation for laundering operations connected to drug trade and human trafficking.
- The Judiciary and Intelligence Agencies ceased to function as legal arbiters, instead operating as shields for criminal elites.
- Cultural Diplomacy, from children's propaganda to religious centers, advanced foreign ideological entrenchment.

The result is a geopolitical anomaly: a state that is both a satellite of external actors and a central exporter of organized chaos.

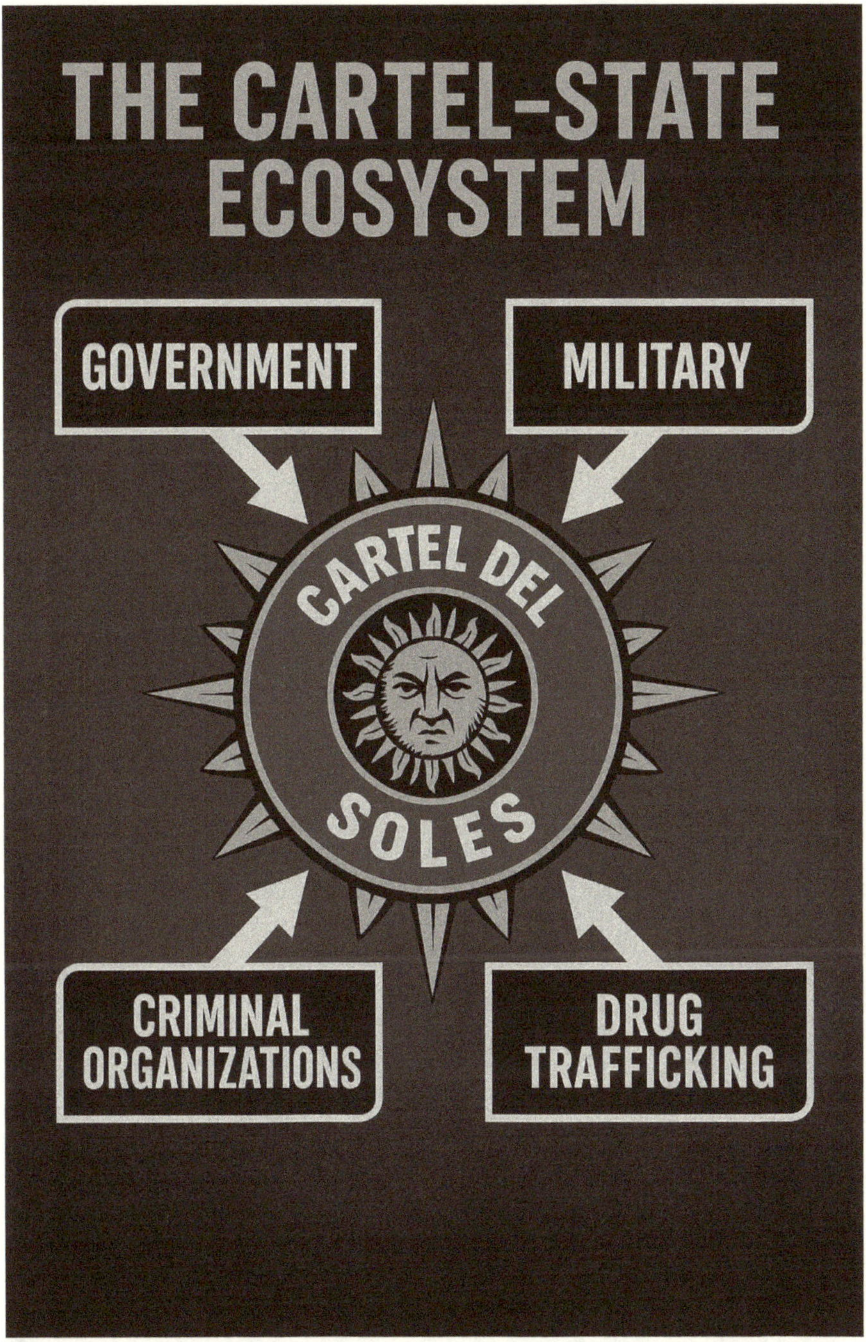

THE CARTEL-STATE ECOSYSTEM

- GOVERNMENT
- MILITARY
- CRIMINAL ORGANIZATIONS
- DRUG TRAFFICKING

CARTEL DEL SOLES

Closing Reflection: The Venezuela Prototype

What Venezuela has become is no longer simply a failed state — it is a prototypical convergence model for authoritarian criminal regimes of the future. It proves that governance structures can be hijacked not merely by ideology or authoritarianism, but by transnational criminal rationality aligned with global hybrid interests.

What happens in Venezuela does not stay in Venezuela.

The next chapter will examine the global reverberations of this prototype — from subversive diplomacy in Europe to state infiltration in Africa and the Americas.

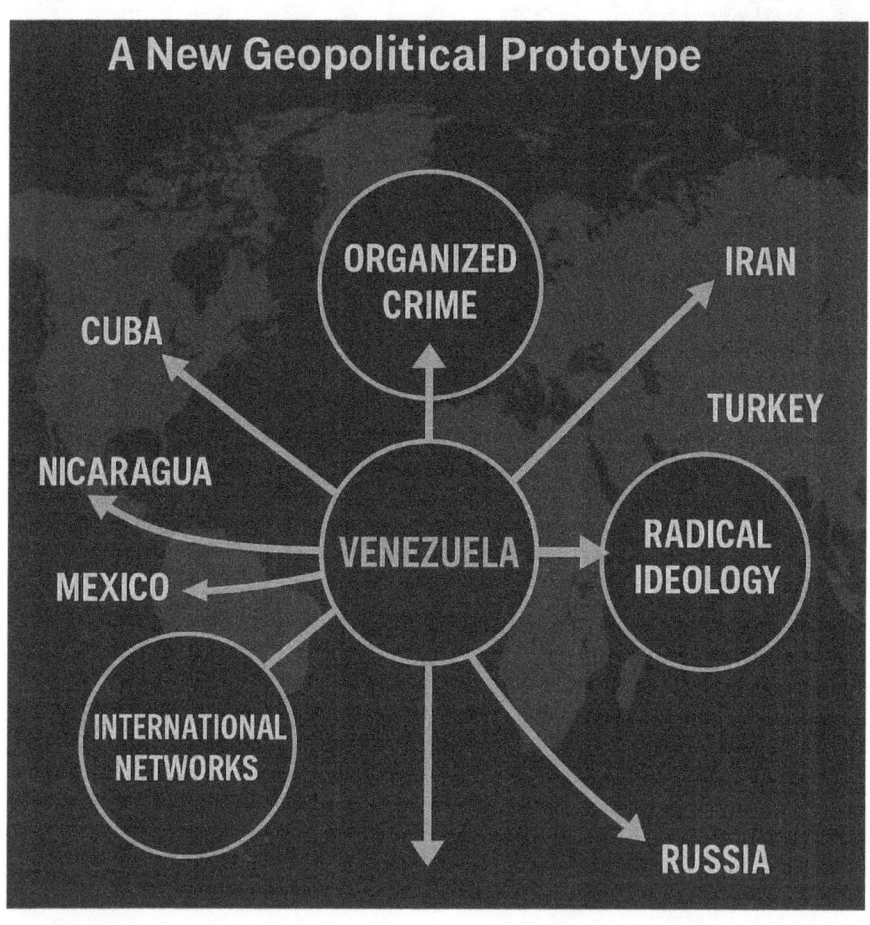

Narco-State and the Ecosystem of Power – The Consolidation of a Transnational Regime

A Criminal System Structured from Within the State: The Convergence of Political Power, Military Forces, Illicit Economies, and International Ideological Networks

As Nicolás Maduro's regime evolved, what was once viewed as a flawed or populist state apparatus has morphed into a meticulously organized transnational criminal architecture. Venezuela is no longer merely a collapsed state; it is a Cartel-State ecosystem, where state actors, drug cartels, terrorist organizations, geopolitical allies (Iran, Russia, Cuba), and multiple illicit economies converge and cooperate.

1. From Government to Cartel-Government

The Venezuelan regime cannot be understood through traditional frameworks of public administration or authoritarianism. It now functions as a Cartel-Government Hybrid—a structure that fuses formal governance with the operational logic of organized crime. This transformation has enabled:

• Control of drug trafficking through military units, especially the Cartel de los Soles within the National Guard;

• Use of PDVSA as a platform for money laundering, human trafficking, and criminal finance;

• Strategic alliances with Hezbollah, ELN, FARC remnants, and extremist cells across the region;

• The export of gold, coltan, and strategic minerals via illicit routes under diplomatic cover.

2. Institutionalized Criminality

The Venezuelan bureaucratic apparatus has become a facade for systematic criminal operations. Ministries, consulates, state-owned companies, and even social programs function as tools for influence trafficking, asset laundering, and funding of covert networks.

Through constitutional reforms, decrees, and parallel institutions (e.g., ANC, communal councils), the regime has embedded impunity into the legal structure. The judiciary and legislature have been fully co-opted to shield the criminal elite.

3. Militarized Corruption and Loyal Complicity

The Venezuelan armed forces have been deeply corrupted and transformed into enforcers of the criminal order. In exchange for financial incentives, territory control, and illicit business franchises, high-ranking officers have pledged loyalty to the regime.
- The Cartel de los Soles operates as a shadow command structure within the military.
- U.S. indictments have identified generals involved in drug trafficking, terrorism, and crimes against humanity.
- A system of selective privilege and intimidation ensures institutional obedience.

4. Illicit Financial Infrastructure

With oil revenue in decline and the formal economy dismantled, the regime has built a robust criminal financial ecosystem, including:
- Global money laundering via offshore banks, shell companies, crypto assets;
- Illegal gold exports and mineral extraction through criminal syndicates;
- Currency manipulation schemes and opaque deals with sanctioned countries.

Financial intelligence estimates that 30–40% of Venezuela's GDP now originates from illicit sources.

5. Parallel Diplomacy and Geopolitical Shielding

The Venezuelan regime benefits from an international support network, comprising:
- Iran – financial logistics, ideological coordination, technical training;
- Cuba – state intelligence services, internal control mechanisms, strategic advisory;
- Russia – arms deals, cyber infrastructure, cryptocurrency facilitation;
- Hezbollah – regional presence, smuggling routes, ideological propagation.

Together, these actors form a hostile geopolitical axis that undermines Western influence in the region and protects the regime from isolation.

Regional Fallout – The Export of Criminal Governance

How Venezuela's Cartel-State Model Is Infecting the Hemisphere

The Venezuelan crisis is no longer confined within its borders. The criminal governance model built by the Maduro regime is now being exported across Latin America and the Caribbean, reshaping regional dynamics in ways that threaten sovereignty, security, and democratic institutions.

1. Geopolitical Spillover

The infiltration of Venezuelan actors into neighboring countries has catalyzed instability:
- In Colombia, dissident FARC and ELN guerrillas operate with logistical and military support from Venezuelan territory.
- In Brazil, border regions like Roraima have become hubs for illegal mining, arms trafficking, and refugee exploitation linked to Venezuelan criminal cells.
- In Ecuador and Peru, surging migration has created vulnerabilities exploited by cartels and extremist recruiters.

Venezuela has become both a refuge and a projection base for multiple non-state armed actors.

2. Tren de Aragua – The Transnational Terrorist-Criminal Franchise

Perhaps the clearest example of criminal export is the rise of Tren de Aragua, a Venezuelan-born gang that has expanded operations across:
- Colombia
- Chile
- Peru
- Ecuador
- Argentina
- Brazil
- Panama
- Spain

Tren de Aragua embodies a new form of hybridized narco-structure: part prison gang, part transnational criminal organization. Its activities include:
- Human trafficking and sexual exploitation;
- Arms smuggling;
- Extortion and digital fraud;
- Kidnapping and territorial control.

The group has become a mirror of the Venezuelan regime's internal structure, fusing hierarchy, ideology, and brutal enforcement.

Note: Interpol, regional intelligence agencies, and multiple police forces now classify Tren de Aragua as a "high-risk transnational threat."

3. Political Contagion: The Rise of Proxy Regimes

The "Bolivarian model" has inspired or enabled the emergence of ideologically aligned governments that replicate aspects of Venezuela's system:

- Nicaragua under Daniel Ortega has adopted similar patterns of repression, electoral fraud, and external criminal partnerships.
- Bolivia under the MAS party has sustained links with coca networks and regional leftist coordination.
- Some Caribbean nations serve as financial intermediaries or diplomatic shields for Venezuelan operations.

This political contagion amplifies the difficulty of isolating the criminal regime diplomatically.

4. Criminal Integration of Migrant Routes

Mass displacement from Venezuela—more than 8 million people—has created a multi-layered vulnerability zone stretching from the Andes to the U.S. southern border.

Criminal organizations exploit refugee routes to:
- Recruit vulnerable individuals into trafficking operations;
- Insert sleeper agents for extortion networks;
- Smuggle narcotics under the guise of humanitarian caravans.

The migration crisis, thus, is not merely humanitarian—it is a security vector deliberately weaponized by criminal-political structures.

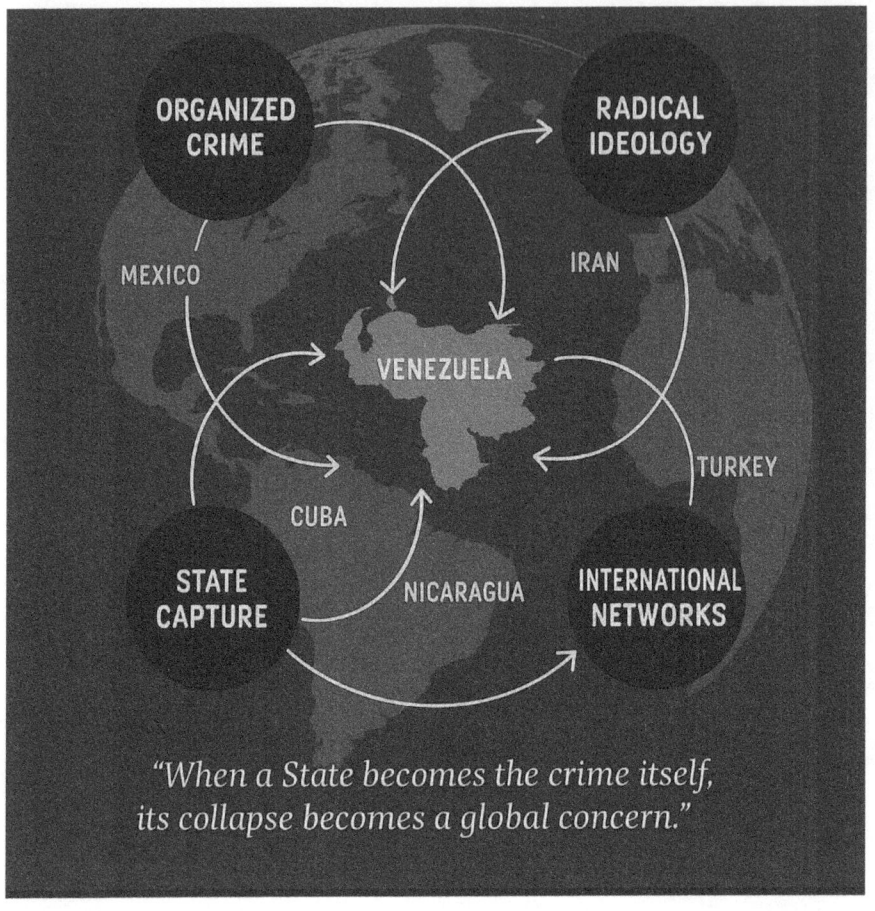

THE SHADOW MANDATE: The Legacy of a Narco-State and the Challenge of Truth

Introduction: A Nation Taken Over

Venezuela is not only a nation in crisis; it is today a state redesigned as an operational platform for transnational crime, covert terrorism, and ideological engineering. Unlike other countries mired in corruption, in Venezuela, crime has become institutionalized. The Maduro regime, heir to Hugo Chávez's project, has not only consolidated a network of political, military, and economic control; it has internationalized the threat.

The State as a Criminal Platform

What was once a republican state now functions as a transnational criminal hub. The Cartel of the Suns does not operate in the shadows: it operates from ministries, embassies, military commands, and PDVSA offices. The synergy between public officials, senior military commanders, and criminal groups has produced a new type of governance: criminal governance with international reach.

The Foreign Deployment: The Exportation of the Criminal Model

The Venezuelan diaspora is not only a human tragedy, it is also a political instrument. From Spain to Chile, from the United States to Mexico, structures linked to Chavismo are linked to cells of the Tren de Aragua, illicit financial networks, and ideological operators. The export of the Venezuelan criminal model constitutes a hemispheric threat.

The Internationalization of Impunity

The failure of organizations such as the UN, the OAS, and the International Criminal Court has allowed Maduro and his allies to operate with impunity. Despite detailed reports of systematic human rights violations, torture, forced disappearances, and extrajudicial executions, the international system remains captured by diplomatic rhetoric.

A Systemic and Evolving Threat

What we are witnessing is not just another dictatorship. It is a new architecture of criminal power with false legitimacy, combining revolutionary language, the tools of the state, and the cover of international alliances like Iran, Russia, Turkey, and networks like Hezbollah. It is a hybrid, systemic, and expanding threat.

The Call: Document, Denounce, Awaken

This chapter is not simply an exercise in denunciation. It is an ethical mandate. Documenting this process means resisting oblivion. It means honoring the victims. It means drawing a map for future generations and legal structures that will one day be held accountable. Silence is not an option.

Chapter 4
SEEDS OF SUSPICION. The Birth of a Narco-Terrorist State and Its Hemispheric Expansion

"The Born of a Narco-Regime"

By Johan Obdola

"Deep within the shadows, where darkness holds dominion,
A regime of narco-terrorism establishes its roots.
Like a creature born from the chains of greed and power,
It silently thrives, hidden from view.

From its very core, a nation is consumed
By corruption's insidious tendrils.
Where justice fades, the once vibrant colours of virtue
Become a distant memory,
As despair tightens its grip and hope vanishes.

From whispered deals in secret halls
To blood-stained streets where fear holds sway,
The narco-terror regime enthralls,
With promises of power's endless play.

Through violence's grip and terror's song,
It tightens its grasp, unyielding and strong.
Innocence is lost, amid the throng,
As darkness spreads, the shadows prolong.

Yet still, a flicker, a spark of light,
In hearts that yearn for freedom's flight.
Against the tide, they stand and fight,
To break the chains of narco's might.

So let us rise, with courage true,
To stem the tide of darkness' brew.
For in the face of tyranny's view,

We'll build a world where justice rings anew."

The Genesis of a Narco-Regime: Strategic Foundations and Geopolitical Engineering

The genesis of the Chavista revolution marked a pivotal rupture in Venezuela's political and historical trajectory — not merely the rise of a populist leader, but the inception of a regime that would come to redefine the architecture of criminal governance in the Western Hemisphere.

At the heart of this transformation lay a volatile convergence of forces: political disillusionment, social fatigue, institutional decay, geopolitical opportunism, and transnational criminal infiltration. Venezuela — once a nation rich in strategic resources and blessed with a privileged geolocation — stood at a precarious intersection between immense potential and existential peril.

A Strategic Geography, A Fractured State

As neighbouring Colombia grappled with the surge of narcotrafficking empires, Venezuela's porous borders and fragile institutions became vulnerable to exploitation. The country's vast oil wealth, weak judicial oversight, and compromised law enforcement structures created the ideal ecosystem for criminal incubation.

The shifting geopolitical landscape at the end of the Cold War — with its collapsing binaries and emergent multipolarity — offered the perfect stage for a new kind of state actor to emerge. It was not one defined by ideology alone, but by its willingness to weaponize ideology, corruption, and chaos for the consolidation of absolute power.

Cuba: The Shadow Ally

In this ideological and strategic vacuum, Cuba became a critical architect behind Venezuela's revolutionary pivot. More than just a partner, Havana became the tutor.

Cuban intelligence operatives, military advisors, and political tacticians embedded themselves into the core of the Venezuelan state, transforming its security and intelligence apparatus into a mirror of the Cuban model: centralized, repressive, and ideologically militant.

Together, Caracas and Havana envisioned a hemispheric axis of defiance — one that would serve as a sanctuary for dissidents, criminals, terrorists, and radical actors opposed to the Western liberal order.

A Calculated Coup of the State

This was no spontaneous uprising. The Bolivarian revolution was meticulously engineered over years, deploying a sophisticated matrix of social manipulation, populist rhetoric, paramilitary infiltration, and electoral deception. Widespread discontent and systemic corruption were not just exploited — they were cultivated.

The revolution's architects, adept at cultivating chaos, understood that the disintegration of state institutions would create a vacuum. Into that void, they inserted a new logic of power: the narco-terrorist logic — where state actors, guerrilla networks, criminal syndicates, and foreign regimes operated under a shared umbrella of impunity.

Venezuela: The New Criminal Nexus

From the ashes of the republic emerged a new kind of state — a Cartel-State — one that no longer differentiated between governance and crime. In this emerging order, Venezuela became a geopolitical hub for transnational threat actors: a convergence zone for drug cartels, Hezbollah operatives, Iranian proxies, and corrupt military elites.

Rather than confronting criminality, the state fused with it. What emerged was a hybrid regime that weaponized sovereignty, manipulated humanitarian crises, and expanded its influence through illicit financial flows, ideological networks, and strategic migration engineering.

The Death of Governance, the Birth of Threat

The collapse of traditional governance in Venezuela marked more than a national tragedy — it heralded the rise of a prototype for criminal insurgency cloaked in state legitimacy. As non-state actors gained power globally, Venezuela stood at the vanguard, becoming the world's first fully operational narco-terrorist state with transcontinental projection.

Its model — combining populist language, state complicity, foreign alliances, and institutional capture — became a blueprint for other rogue actors seeking to erode the Western-led international order from within.

The Shadow Nexus: Narco-Trafficking, Terrorism, and the Strategic Reengineering of Venezuela

Geography as a Weaponized Asset

Venezuela's strategic geographic location — encompassing a vast Caribbean coastline, unguarded land borders, and direct access to major maritime and aerial routes — has transformed the country into a linchpin of global narcotrafficking. Initially operating as a logistical corridor for Colombian cartels, the Venezuelan state, under Chavista rule, evolved from passive facilitator to active partner in a transnational criminal architecture.

Early collaborations with the Revolutionary Armed Forces of Colombia (FARC) and the National Liberation Army (ELN) forged a mutually beneficial relationship: narcotics for transit, protection for power. These alliances cemented the country's role as a bridge between insurgency and organized crime, setting the foundation for an increasingly complex and lethal network.

Over time, this shadow alliance expanded, incorporating actors such as the Sinaloa Cartel, Hezbollah, and state actors aligned with Iran, Russia, and other rogue regimes.

What began as a corridor became a convergence zone — where drug lords, terrorists, corrupt politicians, and foreign operatives operate under the umbrella of state protection.

Corruption as Operational Doctrine

Institutional corruption in Venezuela is no longer a symptom — it is a system. The country's security forces, judiciary, and intelligence services have been hollowed out, reconfigured to serve as the operational arms of a criminal state. Bribery, coercion, and political protection are now currencies of governance. High-ranking officials — many under international sanctions — actively facilitate trafficking, money laundering, and arms transfers.

The corrosive power of narco-money has reached every level of government. From municipal offices to ministerial cabinets, Venezuela's political ecosystem functions under the influence of illicit finance. Criminality is no longer hidden — it is institutionalized, legitimized, and exported.

The Terror-Narco Convergence

The regime's relationship with global terrorist entities marks one of the most alarming developments of the Chavista era. Venezuela is now a sanctuary and operational platform for extremist groups, particularly Hezbollah and other proxies aligned with Iran's Islamic Revolutionary Guard Corps (IRGC). This alignment is not rhetorical — it is logistical, financial, and ideological.

> Inside Venezuela, Hezbollah maintains networks engaged in:
> - Money laundering operations via shell companies and black-market exchanges
> - Arms trafficking, often routed through state-controlled ports and airstrips
> - Recruitment and ideological propaganda in sympathetic zones

This terror-narco hybrid has elevated Venezuela from a regional crisis to a global threat vector, one that transcends drug policy and reaches into the core of international counterterrorism and intelligence frameworks.

A Catalyst for Hemispheric Instability

The implications of this criminal-terrorist nexus are profound. Venezuela has become a launchpad for destabilization throughout the hemisphere. The unchecked flow of drugs, weapons, and illicit capital undermines neighboring states — particularly in Colombia, Ecuador, Brazil, Peru, Mexico, and Central America — while simultaneously sowing chaos in urban centers across Europe and the U.S.

This chaos is not accidental. It is part of a deliberate strategy: to fragment regional governance, destabilize democratic regimes, and expand the reach of a criminal-political ideology cloaked in anti-imperial rhetoric but fueled by illicit economies.

The Collapse of Sovereignty and the Call for Global Response

Venezuela's transformation has redefined the very concept of statehood. It is no longer merely a failed state — it is an engineered narco-terrorist regime, operating with the protection of international alliances and the negligence (or complicity) of global institutions.

Its role in enabling the spread of terrorism, radicalization, and narco-trafficking demands more than rhetorical condemnation. It requires:
- Unified multilateral responses through coordinated sanctions, intelligence operations, and security alliances
- Designation mechanisms for criminal states under international law
- Proactive civic movements and media exposure to counter disinformation and ideological subversion

Moreover, Venezuela's documented support for terrorist organizations — including, but not limited to, Hezbollah and Iranian-aligned proxies — introduces a further layer of complexity to the regional and global security matrix. The growing nexus between narco-trafficking and terrorism financing raises alarm over the accelerated diffusion of radical ideologies and extremist activities across Latin America.

This symbiotic relationship between terrorist entities and narco-trafficking networks is not incidental; it is systemic. It amplifies the magnitude and multiplicity of threats, creating an operational environment in which violent extremism is not only tolerated, but weaponized. As Venezuela increasingly serves as an ideological and logistical safe haven, the pathways for radicalization, training, and recruitment are expanding — posing deep challenges for law enforcement, intelligence, and civil society across the Americas.

In essence, the convergence of terrorism and narco-criminality within Venezuela constitutes a direct assault on the collective security architecture of the Western Hemisphere. It is no longer a Venezuelan crisis — it is a hemispheric emergency. Addressing this evolving threat requires nothing short of a strategic realignment among democratic nations: one that prioritizes intelligence coordination, judicial accountability, regional security frameworks, and the dismantling of state-sponsored criminal regimes.

Failure to act decisively will perpetuate a cycle of violence, impunity, and regional fragmentation, undermining not only the prospects for peace in Latin America but also the credibility of the international system tasked with upholding it.

The Narco-Terrorist Chavista Revolution Goes to Latin America

"Alerta, alerta que camina... la espada de Bolívar por América Latina."

"Alert, alert, the sword of Bolívar walks through Latin America."

This chant, echoed in rallies from Caracas to Buenos Aires, is more than ideological fervor. It is the symbolic expression of a criminal and political export model: the Chavista Revolution—weaponized, radicalized, and metastasizing throughout Latin America.

From Coup Plotter to Populist Messiah

The ascent of Hugo Chávez was neither accidental nor democratic in its origins. It emerged from the shadows of two violent coup attempts in 1992 that redefined Venezuela's political trajectory.

The first, known as Operation Zamora, took place on February 4, 1992. A coordinated insurrection led by five Venezuelan Army lieutenant colonels—Hugo Chávez Frías, Francisco Arias Cárdenas, Yoel Acosta Chirinos, Jesús Miguel Ortiz Contreras, and Jesús Urdaneta—targeted the constitutional government of President Carlos Andrés Pérez. Although the rebellion spread across key cities (Caracas, Maracaibo, Valencia, and Maracay), it ultimately failed, and the conspirators were imprisoned.

Just nine months later, on November 27, 1992, a second coup attempt was launched. This time, it involved both military and civilian factions, aiming to capture President Pérez and install a "civic-military junta." One parallel objective was the liberation of Hugo Chávez from prison. The outcome was catastrophic: over 350 Venezuelans were killed across both uprisings.

Despite this bloody legacy, Chávez would reemerge not in handcuffs, but in a presidential sash. In 1998, he was elected president, riding a wave of disenchantment with traditional parties and widespread socio-economic frustration. His inauguration on January

17, 1999, fresh from a visit to Cuba, marked the beginning of a radical and irreversible transformation.

From the moment he took office, Chávez sought to undermine the existing democratic order. In his inaugural speech, he dismissed the legitimacy of the 1961 Constitution and quickly invoked the "Constituent Power" to rewrite the constitutional framework—an act not of reform, but of political rupture.

The Birth of a Populist-Criminal Blueprint

The first three years of Chávez's rule were characterized by the rapid construction of a loyalist structure, designed not only to consolidate power internally but to export revolution externally. With charismatic populism, strategic alliances, and a carefully orchestrated messaging campaign, Chávez began to position himself as a "criollo messiah"—a savior for the oppressed, a warrior against imperialism, and a visionary with a Bolivarian mission.

But beneath the revolutionary rhetoric lay a blueprint for state capture:
- Radical populism to manipulate the masses
- Institutional corruption to dismantle checks and balances
- Strategic use of crime and terrorism as tools of control and intimidation
- Alliances with rogue regimes and non-state actors to project power beyond borders

This formula would later become a template for hemispheric expansion, replicated and refined in countries such as Nicaragua, Bolivia, and Argentina, with operational ties extending as far as Mexico, Colombia, and the Caribbean.

Even after Hugo Chávez's death on March 5, 2013, large segments of Venezuela's most vulnerable population began to venerate him as a quasi-spiritual figure. His image adorned altars across barrios, surrounded by candles and santería rituals—practices that Chávez himself had encouraged, adapting Cuban syncretic religiosity into a tool of mass manipulation and devotion. He had transcended the role of president; he became a cultic symbol, a "sacred leader" whose revolutionary mythos was weaponized even after his demise.

But long before that, Chávez had begun the systematic transformation of the Venezuelan state. As early as 2005, he launched a comprehensive strategy aimed at achieving near-absolute control over national institutions. This included:

• Politicizing the Armed Forces, turning them into a militarized wing of the Bolivarian Revolution.

• Dismantling constitutional principles and the separation of powers.

• Creating a culture of institutional penetration, using intimidation, corruption, and promises of immunity to secure loyalty across all sectors.

This radical transformation cemented Chávez's role as "Caudillo of the Revolution"—a figure whose strength came not only from charisma, but from calculated repression and strategic alliances with global criminal networks.

Anti-Americanism as Geopolitical Doctrine

Central to Chávez's worldview was an intense hostility toward the United States, meticulously cultivated under the mentorship of Fidel Castro. Castro acted as both spiritual godfather and tactical advisor, ensuring that Venezuela's revolution followed Cuba's playbook of anti-capitalist radicalization—while ironically embracing the luxuries and benefits of capitalist wealth for themselves and their elites.

This ideological hypocrisy—raging against Western imperialism while exploiting its mechanisms for personal enrichment—became a model replicated across the Bolivarian alliance. The term "Dictatorship of the Extreme Left" came to define this political model: one built on populist rhetoric, iron-fisted control, and transnational criminal collaboration. Venezuela under Chávez was its most dangerous prototype.

The Expulsion of the DEA and the Welcome of the Cartels

A defining moment came in 2005, when Chávez expelled the U.S. Drug Enforcement Administration (DEA) from Venezuela. This move symbolized a deliberate shift: from a state cooperating (however superficially) in anti-drug efforts, to one becoming a strategic command center for narco-trafficking and global criminal coordination.

This action opened the floodgates for:
- The operational entry of Hezbollah, Iran's Quds Force, and the FARC.
- The gradual integration of Mexican cartels, particularly the Sinaloa Cartel, which became the Chavista regime's primary narco-partner after the FARC.

As Chávez publicly condemned U.S. "imperialism," he was quietly constructing a narco-state, providing sanctuary and operational space to extremist groups, criminal syndicates, corrupt businessmen, and rogue regimes. Venezuela was now positioned as a transnational hub for ideological and criminal convergence.

The Rapid Deepening of Criminal Alliances

By 2010, a marked influx of foreign operatives was underway. Agents from FARC, ELN, Hezbollah, and the Sinaloa Cartel were not only welcomed—they were integrated. Venezuela's territory became an unregulated corridor for drug trafficking, weapons smuggling, and terrorist financing.

This consolidation served a dual strategic objective:
1. Secure financing for the revolution, ensuring liquidity for political control.
2. Criminalize the state from within, fostering loyalty through complicity and mutual benefit.

This phase was characterized by the vertical alignment of organized crime with state functions, and the erosion of any remaining legal or civic restraints.

The Rise of the Cartel de los Soles and the Role of Iran

Between 2004 and 2008, Diosdado Cabello, one of the regime's most powerful figures, consolidated control over the Cartel de los Soles—the Venezuelan military-linked drug cartel that would become the regime's most powerful illicit arm. Under his leadership, the cartel evolved into an institutionalized narco-military enterprise, operating with full impunity.

Meanwhile, Tareck El Aissami, a key Chavista insider, was tasked by Chávez to formalize operational ties with the Islamic Republic of Iran. His role included:
- Facilitating the infiltration of the Quds Force into the Venezuelan military and civil society.
- Establishing permanent structures for Hezbollah's operations within Venezuelan territory.

This Iran–Venezuela axis would go on to form a strategic partnership, centred on ideological alignment, shared anti-Americanism, and the pursuit of asymmetric power through terrorism, proxy networks, and the drug trade.

By expelling the U.S. Drug Enforcement Administration (DEA) in 2005, Hugo Chávez signaled a strategic realignment: Venezuela was no longer a reluctant participant in the war on drugs—it was becoming its antagonist. Behind this geopolitical maneuver, Chávez was preparing the ground for the active presence of Iran's Quds Force, Hezbollah, the FARC, and the Sinaloa Cartel, among others. This shift was not theoretical—it was operational, deliberate, and irreversible.

This initial phase caught many sectors of Venezuelan civil society off guard. Chávez, once perceived as a charismatic populist with reformist potential, had carefully crafted a persona of accessibility and national renewal. However, as his agenda unfolded, Venezuelans found themselves torn between hope and betrayal—enticed by promises, yet unaware of the criminal architecture being embedded beneath the surface.

By 2010, the influx of agents, operatives, and logistical representatives from FARC, ELN, and Mexican drug cartels—most notably the Sinaloa Cartel—was no longer speculative. Venezuela had become a strategic corridor and operational hub for hemispheric and global narco-trafficking. The Sinaloa Cartel, second only to FARC during the early years, became the regime's most trusted criminal partner.

This convergence was not accidental. It served clear, dual purposes:

1. To secure massive illicit funding for the expansion and sustainability of the Chavista revolution.

2. To institutionalize corruption, criminal loyalty, and social control, creating a system where participation in crime became the primary path to political and economic advancement.

Between 2004 and 2008, Diosdado Cabello, one of the regime's most feared enforcers, consolidated control over the Cartel de los Soles—the military-linked drug trafficking syndicate that would soon dominate Venezuela's criminal landscape. At the same time, Tareck El Aissami, acting under Chávez's direct mandate, was entrusted with deepening ties with the Islamic Republic of Iran, establishing Quds Force and Hezbollah cells within Venezuela's military structure and wider civil society.

Exporting the Revolution: A Transnational Offensive

Beginning in 2010, Chávez launched a transnational expansion plan for his revolution. This initiative unfolded in phases and zones of influence, and was executed through a network of Cuban, Venezuelan, and later Iranian operatives deployed to countries including Colombia, Argentina, Brazil, Mexico, Panama, El Salvador, Nicaragua, and others.

The objectives of these operatives were multifaceted:
- To ensure the personal protection of sympathetic political leaders.
- To infiltrate and co-opt local social movements and political parties.
- To propagate revolutionary ideology using state-funded programs and psychological operations.

Simultaneously, these agents constructed operational networks intertwined with terrorist entities, including:
- Venezuelan state intelligence agencies (SEBIN and DGCIM).
- Iranian operatives and Quds Force liaisons.
- Hezbollah's external security apparatus.

Once operational footholds were secured, these networks expanded publicly and covertly, enabling the regime to project influence well beyond Latin America. Today, these structures are active in North America (USA, Canada), the Caribbean, Africa, Europe (notably Spain and Portugal), the Middle East, and parts of Asia.

This expansion of criminal diplomacy and proxy warfare has redefined Venezuela's role in global geopolitics—not as a failed state, but as a conscious exporter of instability, ideology, and organized crime.

The Price of Power: The Human Toll of a Criminal Revolution

The true cost of the Chavista Revolution cannot be measured in policy shifts or political slogans—it must be reckoned in human suffering, death, and destruction.

- Over 9,700 Venezuelans were killed by Maduro's armed revolutionary forces by 2023, including more than 2,700 extrajudicial executions.
- An estimated 40,351 violations of personal integrity—including torture, physical abuse, and degrading treatment—have been documented under the Maduro regime.
- During the 15,000+ protests between 2003 and 2020, approximately 450 demonstrators were killed by state forces.

Perhaps most staggering: an estimated 480,000 people have been killed in Venezuela over 25 years as a result of:
- Extreme levels of violence and crime.
- Judicial impunity and lawlessness.
- The destruction of public security institutions.

Only in recent years—due in part to the massive exodus of Venezuelans abroad—have homicide rates shown relative decline.

A Revolution of Ruin: The Collapse of a Nation, The Export of a Threat

This is not merely the consequence of a failed political model. It is the calculated result of a state-engineered project—one that leveraged narco-trafficking, terrorism, and authoritarian control to establish one of the most destructive regimes in modern Western Hemispheric history.

After twenty-five years in power, the so-called Bolivarian Revolution has delivered no tangible achievement—only a legacy of devastation. A simple review of national and international headlines reflects this grim consensus:

"Repression, poverty, corruption, and exile"
"Twenty-five years of Chavismo—or billions of dollars stolen"
"The hegemonic project of endless crises"
"The utopia that opened the doors to hell"
"Youth only know dictatorship"
"25 years of economic disaster"
"The creation of a State of Destruction"
"A quarter-century of setbacks and impositions under Chavista power"

One of the most emblematic signs of Venezuela's collapse is the implosion of its once-proud oil industry. Petróleos de Venezuela, S.A. (PDVSA)—once the economic engine of the nation—has disintegrated. In 1998, PDVSA produced 3.3 million barrels of oil per day. Today, it barely exceeds 796,000 barrels per day, according to OPEC. Mismanagement, corruption, and the politicization of operations gutted the industry.

But the damage is not limited to oil. Across state-owned sectors—petrochemicals, electricity, water, mining, agriculture, and telecommunications—corruption and operational collapse have become systemic. According to Transparencia Venezuela's 2018 report on State-Owned Enterprises, most of the country's 526 public companies provide no service, no benefit—only cost and decay.

The so-called 21st Century Socialism model, built on expropriation, price controls, and command economics, has obliterated Venezuela's private sector. Between 1998 and 2019, more than 60% of all private companies ceased to exist. The result? A shattered economy that has shrunk to one-third its size in 1999.

Non-oil exports have plummeted from $7.1 billion to just $3 billion in 2021. Ricardo Hausmann of Harvard's Growth Lab notes that Venezuela's economic complexity now ranks among the world's lowest—comparable to East Timor, Eritrea, Chad, and Djibouti.

A Human Exodus and the Collapse of National Capacity

More than nine million Venezuelans—approximately 28% of the population—have fled the country in the last 25 years. This is one of the largest mass displacements in the world.

The loss of human capital is irreversible. The aging population, brain drain, and destruction of families have obliterated the nation's workforce and social fabric. Venezuela is now a broken country—socially fragmented, economically collapsed, and strategically hijacked.

Phase Two: The Transnationalization of the Chavista Model

The second stage of the revolution's export began in 2015, though its organizational architecture had been in development for over a decade. With guidance from Fidel Castro, Venezuela implemented a sub-regional cell-based structure across Latin America and parts of the Southern Hemisphere.

Castro was not only a master of revolutionary manipulation, but also the architect of what can be described as a "Doctrine of Collective Idiotism": a system that deconstructs formal education, distorts social knowledge, and replaces civic literacy with radical indoctrination. His tactics, adapted for poor and corrupt nations, sowed ideological control through misinformation and dependency.

Castro taught Chávez that populist manipulation and revolutionary infiltration are most effective in fragile states—where democratic institutions are weak, poverty is high, and accountability is absent.

The strategy was clear: export the revolution to key countries—Colombia, Argentina, Brazil, Mexico, Panama, El Salvador, and beyond—using ideology, criminal networks, and covert operations. Under Cuban mentorship and with Iranian assistance, Venezuela became the geopolitical bridgehead of a hemispheric subversion campaign.

Latin America: Testing Ground of the Chavista Narco-Revolution

Latin America has long been a region of political experimentation and socio-economic volatility. Between 2010 and 2014, it became a laboratory for the transnational expansion of the Chavista Revolution—a radical, populist, and ultimately criminal geopolitical movement born in Venezuela under Hugo Chávez, influenced by Fidel Castro, and later manipulated by Raúl Castro, the Cuban Revolutionary Committee, Iran, Russia, and a loose alliance of extremist regimes and ideological militias.

What was presented as a revolutionary model advocating for economic justice, popular empowerment, and anti-imperialism, quickly evolved into a front for narco-terrorism, authoritarianism, and regional destabilization.

The Chavista model promised to redistribute wealth, empower the marginalized, and overthrow entrenched elites. But behind this narrative lay a deeper formula—a deliberate indoctrination strategy rooted in what may be described as collective idiotism: the mass manipulation of public consciousness through a mix of populist rhetoric, militarized nationalism, and the romanticization of revolutionary violence. This formula proved dangerously effective in winning the support of impoverished and disenfranchised communities, not only in Venezuela but across the region.

The Region as a Narco-Terrorist Battlefield

Latin America's pre-existing vulnerabilities—organized crime, the drug trade, paramilitary structures, and fragile democratic institutions—offered fertile ground for the Chavista revolution to test and expand its model.

Venezuela, once considered a bastion of democratic modernity in South America, became the epicenter of a new geopolitical experiment that deliberately fused criminal operations with state power. This was not just another ideological shift—it was the institutionalization of narco-terrorism as a mechanism of governance.

Throughout the region, the model found resonance. Populist leaders, often allied with criminal networks, harnessed social grievances to erode checks and balances, undermine the rule of law, and redirect public frustration toward scapegoats: the United States, corporations, the media, and liberal democracy itself.

The Criminal Expansion Model

By the mid-2010s, it became evident that the Venezuelan regime—through its alliances and covert deployments—was engineering a regional network of political and criminal actors that functioned with dual purpose:

1. To consolidate authoritarian control within allied states, using ideological and financial support mechanisms;

2. To establish parallel criminal economies, supported by narcotics, arms trafficking, corruption, and terrorism.

The effect has been catastrophic. The Chavista doctrine exported not just ideas, but operations—embedding agents and financing networks within political parties, trade unions, indigenous movements, and even government structures across Latin America.

A wide array of actors, including the FARC, ELN, Hezbollah, the Quds Force, and Mexican cartels like Sinaloa, found in Venezuela and its allies a safe haven, logistical hub, and ideological partner.

ALBA: The Alliance of Collapse

To formalize its geopolitical ambitions, the Chavista regime created and nurtured ALBA – The Bolivarian Alliance for the Peoples of Our America. Founded in 2004 by Venezuela and Cuba, ALBA was marketed as a counterweight to U.S.-led trade initiatives such as the Free Trade Area of the Americas (FTAA). Its stated aim was to promote regional integration, mutual aid, and anti-imperialist cooperation.

But in practice, ALBA functioned as a political cartel—a coordination mechanism for ideological subversion, financial manipulation, and diplomatic shielding of authoritarian regimes.

Member states—Antigua and Barbuda, Bolivia, Cuba, Dominica, Ecuador, Nicaragua, Saint Lucia, Saint Vincent and the Grenadines, and Venezuela—regularly convened summits not only to discuss regional development, but to strategize against democratic resistance, protect corrupt leaderships, and synchronize narratives.

The bloc provided diplomatic legitimacy to autocracies, facilitated covert operations across borders, and used humanitarian language as a camouflage for transnational criminal alliances.

Institutionalizing Revolution: ALBA, PetroCaribe, and the Chavista Geopolitical Framework

To solidify its regional influence and export the Bolivarian revolution under the guise of "integration and cooperation," Venezuela—under Hugo Chávez's direction and Cuba's guidance—established a series of supranational structures that masked criminal strategy under multilateral diplomacy.

ALBA – A Political Cartel Dressed as Integration

The Bolivarian Alliance for the Peoples of Our America (ALBA), founded in 2004 by Venezuela and Cuba, was publicly promoted as a political and economic alternative to neoliberal trade frameworks like NAFTA and the U.S.-backed FTAA (Free Trade Area of the Americas). Its stated goal was to reduce poverty, promote inclusive development, and empower Latin American nations to reclaim sovereignty from foreign capital.

ALBA offered trade agreements allegedly tailored to the social needs of member states rather than market logic. In 2008, it launched Banco del ALBA, headquartered in Caracas, to fund social and infrastructure projects throughout the bloc. In 2009, the creation of a regional electronic currency, the "sucre" (Sistema Único de Compensación Regional), was introduced to reduce dependency on the U.S. dollar. It was a symbolic and strategic move, referencing Antonio José de Sucre, a key figure in South American independence.

ALBA's long-term ambitions went far beyond finance. It envisioned a unified military force, regional arbitration courts, and expanded social programs in education and health—built around ideological solidarity rather than governance efficiency or rule of law.

Yet beneath this façade, ALBA functioned as a geopolitical shield for authoritarian regimes, a mechanism of ideological coordination, and a vehicle for laundering illicit wealth under the narrative of "solidarity." While some sectors initially supported ALBA's social aims, critics rightly accused it of disrupting legitimate multilateral frameworks such as MERCOSUR, the Andean Community, and CARICOM, and of creating diplomatic protection networks for state-sponsored corruption and transnational crime.

PetroCaribe – Oil Diplomacy Meets Geopolitical Control

In 2005, Chávez launched PetroCaribe, a Venezuela-led oil alliance offering Caribbean and Central American states deeply discounted oil under concessionary financial terms. What seemed like generous economic support was, in truth, a geostrategic bribe—fuel diplomacy exchanged for political alignment and silence.

For over a decade, PetroCaribe allowed Venezuela to purchase influence across the Caribbean while undermining Western-aligned energy initiatives. In 2013, PetroCaribe was linked directly to ALBA, expanding its remit beyond energy to economic integration and ideological alignment.

By 2019, the collapse of Venezuela's oil production—alongside internal corruption and global market fluctuations—caused the PetroCaribe project to disintegrate. Yet in 2022, Saint Vincent and the Grenadines became the first nation to receive Venezuelan oil again under PetroCaribe terms, and in 2023, the Maduro regime declared intentions to revive the program—indicating that oil remains its primary tool of geopolitical coercion.

UNASUR – A Short-Lived Union for Strategic Legitimacy

The Union of South American Nations (UNASUR), launched in 2008, was envisioned as a South American alternative to the Organization of American States (OAS) and NATO-linked institutions. Initially comprising twelve nations, the bloc aimed to create a cohesive platform for regional diplomacy, military cooperation, and continental sovereignty, independent of U.S. influence.

Its founding treaty was signed in Brasília and ratified with legal force in 2011, establishing headquarters in Quito, Ecuador. The project included ambitious plans: a South American Parliament, integrated infrastructure systems, and a regional security council.

Yet UNASUR quickly became a tool for legitimizing authoritarian regimes, particularly Venezuela and Bolivia, and lost credibility among democratic governments. By

2018, disillusionment peaked. Argentina, Brazil, Chile, Colombia, Paraguay, and Peru suspended membership. Colombia and Ecuador formally withdrew in 2018–2019, followed by Uruguay in 2020.

The institution had become paralyzed—its forums descending into propaganda platforms for regimes hostile to liberal democracy. Only recently, in May 2023, Brazil announced it would rejoin UNASUR, under the administration of President Lula da Silva—reviving concerns over its ideological neutrality and future trajectory..

The Regional Response: PROSUR and the Pushback Against the Chavista Regime

By January 2019, regional and international concern had reached a critical threshold regarding Nicolás Maduro's regime and the escalating collapse of Venezuelan democracy. In response to the consolidation of authoritarianism and the geopolitical interference orchestrated by the Bolivarian Revolution, a new counterweight began to take shape.

On March 22, 2019, under the leadership of Chile and Colombia, a new multilateral bloc—PROSUR (Forum for the Progress of South America)—held its inaugural summit in Santiago, Chile. Venezuela was not invited. The deliberate exclusion of the Maduro regime symbolized a rejection of authoritarianism, state-sponsored narco-terrorism, and ideological extremism. Participating nations included Argentina, Brazil, Bolivia, Colombia, Chile, Ecuador, Uruguay, Paraguay, Peru, Guyana, and Suriname, signaling a shift toward institutional recovery, democratic cooperation, and a renewed commitment to regional integrity.

While the long-term coherence and efficacy of PROSUR remain under scrutiny, its formation marked an essential moment: an acknowledgment that traditional organizations like UNASUR, ALBA, and PetroCaribe had been co-opted or weaponized by Chavismo to advance a geopolitical model rooted in manipulation, resource extortion, and ideological blackmail.

Geopolitical Infiltration Through Oil and Ideology

Despite setbacks on the international stage, the Chavista regime continued to wield considerable power through strategic manipulation of regional organizations. Entities like MERCOSUR, ALBA, and PetroCaribe—originally marketed as engines of integration—evolved into mechanisms of institutional control, resource leverage, and intelligence operations. Oil, the regime's most potent tool, was consistently used to bribe political elites, fund loyalist regimes, and penetrate vulnerable democracies across the Caribbean and Latin America.

The ideological project of the Bolivarian Revolution—once camouflaged as social justice—mutated into a transnational criminal alliance, attracting not only radical leftist movements and ideological sympathizers, but also narco-traffickers, extremist groups, corrupt politicians, and internationally sanctioned actors. These alliances were not incidental; they were strategically cultivated to form a continental axis of destabilization, one capable of eroding institutions, undermining civil society, and replacing democratic legitimacy with revolutionary absolutism.

What began as a promise of empowerment for the marginalized has instead produced a multinational framework of chaos, where state failure, insurgency, and impunity intersect. This transformation is no longer theoretical—it is visible in the rise of criminal governance, political repression, and economic disintegration across the hemisphere. From Nicaragua to Bolivia, from the deepening crisis in Haiti to the emboldened populism in parts of South America, the fingerprints of Chavista expansionism are unmistakable.

A Sobering Geopolitical Reality

This is not mere ideological critique, nor is it a partisan narrative. It is a sober geopolitical diagnosis based on decades of accumulated evidence: state capture by organized crime, the militarization of civil society, and the export of revolutionary authoritarianism under the guise of South-South cooperation.

Today, the Chavista Revolution stands as one of the most disruptive forces in the Western Hemisphere. Its operational model—a fusion of populism, crime, and ideological warfare—remains active and dangerous, posing a significant threat to the democratic resilience of Latin America and to global security at large.

The Chavista Narco-Terrorist Regime's Intelligence and Operations Bases in Latin America

The convergence of ideological radicalism, authoritarian governance, and transnational criminal enterprise has transformed Venezuela into the epicenter of hemispheric narco-terrorist network. Spearheaded by Hugo Chávez and expanded by Nicolás Maduro, with sustained influence from Fidel Castro, Raúl Castro, Miguel Díaz-Canel, and Daniel Ortega, this network has embedded itself deeply into the political, military, and intelligence frameworks of Latin America.

Through the fusion of socialism, populism, and criminal opportunism, these regimes have engineered model of state control that sacrifices democracy for power consolidation. The co-optation of institutions, the manipulation of public narratives, and the strategic alliance with global rogue actors notably Iran, China, and Russia—have turned Venezuela and its closest allies into launching pads for covert operations, terrorist logistics, and asymmetric warfare.

The Axis of Authoritarian Symbiosis: Venezuela, Cuba, and Nicaragua

The despotic regimes of Cuba and Nicaragua are not peripheral players. They are core architects and beneficiaries of the Chavista revolutionary export. These states, long plagued by poverty and repression, have found in the Venezuelan regime both a financier and an ideological partner. In return, they provide strategic support, training, and geopolitical cover.

Through this axis, regional infiltration is methodically conducted using tools such as:

Oil-for-loyalty diplomacy (PetroCaribe, ALBA, bilateral deals),
Intelligence integration and base establishment across Latin America,

Covert financing and operational support for terrorist and insurgent groups.

This triangular alliance has enabled a web of subversion that spans not only Latin America and the Caribbean, but reaches deep into Africa, the Middle East, and Europe, with direct implications for national security and continental stability.

Institutional Penetration and Intelligence Footholds

The Chavista regime has used state resources—notably oil revenues and illicit narco proceeds—to bribe political elites, corrupt security sectors, and infiltrate weakened institutions throughout Latin America. Countries with fragile economies and soft governance, particularly in Central America and the Caribbean, have become fertile ground for this asymmetric incursion.

Beyond the obvious figures of Chávez and Maduro, a parallel diplomatic corps has emerged: presidents and former presidents from nations like Argentina, Brazil, and Mexico who lend passive or indirect support to the revolutionary axis. This tacit alliance provides diplomatic legitimacy, obstructs sanctions efforts, and creates fractures within multilateral frameworks like the OAS and CELAC.

The Operational Cartography of the Chavista Intelligence Network

At the core of Venezuela's regional coordination lies an intelligence-military ecosystem commanded by SEBIN (Servicio Bolivariano de Inteligencia Nacional) and DGCIM (Dirección General de Contrainteligencia Militar). These agencies serve as both surveillance tools and operational logistics arms of the narco-terrorist state. Their activities are further amplified by Quds Force elements, Hezbollah cells, and Iranian strategic operatives embedded throughout Venezuela.

From Caracas to the Triple Frontier, from Apure to Margarita Island, this network operates through: Command centers, indoctrination camps, and training schools (often disguised as civic-militar academies or cultural centers), Clandestine supply routes and laundering infrastructures connected to transnational crimina organizations, Logistical hubs that interface directly with guerrilla networks like the ELN and dissident FARC factions.

Underground Warfare Infrastructure: The Caracas Tunnel Network

Between 2016 and 2021, during a classified investigation I led with the support of international intelligence partners, we uncovered a covert subterranean complex built in Caracas. This operationrevealed over 17 kilometers of tunnels constructed by the Chavista regime with Iranian engineering support and Hezbollah logistical oversight.

These tunnels, spanning areas such as:
- Miraflores Palace
- The Central Bank of Venezuela
- Fuerte Tiuna (Military Command HQ)
- Plaza Venezuela
- La Montaña Barracks (where Hugo Chávez's remains rest)

...function as strategic hideouts, arms depots, and command bunkers. Equipped to host up to 1,500 men, these installations hold heavy weaponry, encrypted communications gear, and accommodation units for prolonged siege scenarios. This infrastructure is not symbolic—it is militarily functional, and it remains active and dangerous.

As I disclosed in a joint investigative interview with El Tiempo (Colombia) on April 18, 2020, also attended by Michael Kozak, then U.S. Deputy Assistant Secretary of State for the Western Hemisphere:

"For the past six years, with assistance from Iran and Hezbollah, the regime has constructed underground infrastructure in Caracas. Intelligence estimates confirm approximately 17 kilometers of tunnel networks designed to provide secure movement and entrenchment for elite units in case of foreign intervention or civil conflict."
– Johan Obdola, El Tiempo Interview, from exile in Vancouver, Canada

This network is more than a defensive installation; it represents the entrenchment of a transnational narco-terrorist fortress, one that fuses state power, ideological militancy, and foreign proxies into a single operational doctrine.

Narco-Terrorist Logistics, Forged Identities, and the Strategic Threat from the Triple Frontier

The reach of the Chavista narco-terrorist regime extends far beyond Venezuela's borders. Through a network of proxy actors, forged identities, and transnational criminal alliances, this hybrid apparatus has established operational nodes and intelligence cells across Latin America — with Colombia and the Triple Frontier emerging as focal points of concern.

Colombia: Forged Identities and Hezbollah Infiltration

As early as mid-2019, El Tiempo reported the existence of a mafia entrenched within Colombia's civil registry system, including notaries and official documentation offices. This group, embedded deep within institutional infrastructure, has been selling false identities to foreigners, including Hezbollah operatives. According to sources within U.S. Immigration and Customs Enforcement (ICE) and Migración Colombia, this transnational criminal organization has active branches in at least 12 Colombian departments.

For a fee of up to 20 million Colombian pesos per individual, they issue civil records, ID cards, and passports, facilitating the undetected movement of hostile foreign actors. Payments are often routed through European and Miami-based financial institutions, and the final identities are delivered through clandestine channels to countries such as Venezuela, Turkey, Iraq, Libya, Syria, and Palestine. Notably, these documents are concealed within meat shipments exported from Colombia, a tactic executed via companies with known Hezbollah sponsors.

This is not merely a case of document fraud—it is the systematic subversion of regional sovereignty through the deliberate placement of non-state hostile actors using state-issued credentials.

Margarita Island and the Narco-Terrorist Highway

Within Venezuela, Margarita Island (Nueva Esparta) has long served as a logistical hub for criminal operations. Intelligence gathered during our investigations revealed that Colombian drug cartels, particularly those based in Delta Amacuro, Sucre, Anzoátegui, and the broader eastern coastal zone, have established deep control over these territories. Among the most dominant actors in recent years is the Sinaloa Cartel, which has established an aggressive presence and strategic alliances with remnants of the FARC and elements of the Venezuelan military.

Competition over drug routes leading to Trinidad and Tobago and other Caribbean islands, as staging points for trans-Atlantic shipments to Europe, has ignited inter-cartel and intra-state conflicts. These developments underscore how Venezuela has transitioned from a sovereign state into a staging ground for criminal enterprise and terror logistics.

Clíver Alcalá, Padrino López, and the Shadow Figures of the Revolution

Among the many compromised actors, Clíver Alcalá Cordones stands out as a pivotal figure. Once a top military lieutenant to Nicolás Maduro, Alcalá lived for over a year in Barranquilla, Colombia, before his surrender to U.S. authorities. During his cooperation with U.S. law enforcement, it emerged that his brother, General Carlos Antonio Alcalá Cordones, currently serves as Venezuela's ambassador to Iran, a placement of grave geopolitical consequence.

I previously reported in El Tiempo that Clíver Alcalá played a duplicitous role — purportedly aligning with both Nicolás Maduro and Juan Guaidó — while simultaneously overseeing false flag operations, including the so-called Operation Aurora, orchestrated by Lieutenant José Rodríguez Arana, a Maduro loyalist. These revelations highlight how the regime weaponizes chaos, engineering opposition, and infiltration to mislead both domestic actors and international observers.

Another concerning figure is General Vladimir Padrino López, Venezuela's Defense Minister. Despite being listed by the U.S. government among the regime's most dangerous operatives, the Trump administration notably refrained from placing a reward on his capture. Padrino López's extended family is implicated in numerous real estate and shell company operations in Florida and Texas, including Brisana LLC, Urtaris Realty Group, and Majalud LLC, collectively holding properties valued at over $4 million, according to the Organized Crime and Corruption Reporting Project (OCCRP).

Furthermore, intelligence confirms that the Military Museum in Caracas, which houses the remains of Hugo Chávez and serves as a symbolic temple of the revolution, conceals underground military bases. These subterranean facilities host Hezbollah and Quds Force intelligence centers, constituting a direct threat to regional security and diplomatic stability.

The Triple Frontier: A Tri-National Epicenter of Criminal Convergence

The Triple Frontier — where Argentina, Brazil, and Paraguay converge near Iguazú Falls — represents one of the most strategically dangerous points in the Western Hemisphere. Traditionally a zone of commerce and cultural exchange, it has devolved into a hotbed of illicit activity, exploited by Hezbollah and Iranian networks since the 1990s.

Cities such as Puerto Iguazú (Argentina), Foz do Iguaçu (Brazil), and Ciudad del Este (Paraguay) form the triangular spine of transnational movement, allowing for:
- Terror financing via money laundering through local businesses and charities
- Arms smuggling, forged documentation, and dual citizenship issuance
- Radicalization efforts within diaspora communities
- Smuggling of narcotics and precursor chemicals used in cocaine and heroin processing

These operations are facilitated by corrupt customs officials, criminal syndicates, and the strategic complacency or complicity of political actors in the region. The porous nature of the borders, coupled with weak surveillance infrastructure, allows for near-complete operational freedom for these actors.

The Triple Frontier and the El Aissami Axis: Geopolitical Infiltration and Hybrid Terror

The Triple Frontier, where Argentina, Brazil, and Paraguay converge, has long stood as a crucible of illicit enterprise. From narcotrafficking to arms smuggling, and from counterfeit operations to terror financing, this region has become a hotbed of transnational criminality and terrorist entrenchment, undermining not only regional governance but hemispheric stability.

But the threat is not confined to this tri-national point. The influence of Venezuela's narco-terrorist regime, particularly under the Chavista leadership, has created an ideological and operational extension that stretches directly into the Triple Frontier — activating Hezbollah, Iranian proxies, and criminal allies within Latin America.

Strategic Importance and Global Rivalries

The Triple Frontier's economic relevance and geographic centrality have drawn the attention of both regional powers and global actors. Its porous borders, overlapping jurisdictions, and complex demographics create an ideal terrain for covert operations and asymmetric conflict.

While numerous nations have made efforts to curtail extremist financing and dismantle criminal networks, these initiatives have also revealed the depth and resilience of transnational terror networks embedded in local societies. The success of these networks hinges on political complicity, systemic corruption, and institutional fragility—a dangerous mix that serves the long-term ambitions of the Chavista project and its foreign allies.

The El Aissami Clan: Hezbollah's Venezuelan Bridge

The influence of Tareck El Aissami, a former Venezuelan Vice President and Minister of Petroleum, and his brother Feras El Aissami, is pivotal in understanding the operational connection between Caracas, the Triple Frontier, and the broader Middle East.

According to multiple intelligence reports and investigative sources:
• Tareck El Aissami, of Lebanese and Syrian Druze origin, was appointed by Hugo Chávez as a key interlocutor with Iran and Hezbollah. He has since served in numerous high-level positions, including Governor of Aragua, Minister of Interior and Justice, Vice President, and Minister of Petroleum.
• His brother, Feras El Aissami, has reportedly built a transnational network of shell companies operating in Venezuela, Nicaragua, Mexico, Panama, and the Middle East. These companies allegedly launder narcotics proceeds and finance Hezbollah's activities in Brazil, Argentina, and beyond.
• In 2010, Feras was linked to Walid Makled, one of Venezuela's most notorious drug lords, who publicly stated that he paid Feras $100,000 in exchange for placing an ally in the scientific police of Aragua.

This familial nexus reflects not only the personal merging of state power and criminal enterprise but also the institutional embedding of terrorism financing mechanisms within the Venezuelan regime.

PDVSA-Crypto and the Fall of a Power Broker

In March 2023, Tareck El Aissami was arrested under charges of treason and corruption tied to the PDVSA-Crypto scandal, one of the largest state asset diversion cases in Venezuela's history. Though his arrest was portrayed as a domestic anti-corruption effort, it was in fact the result of an internal power struggle, where Nicolás Maduro handed him over to Diosdado Cabello, his primary rival.

Despite El Aissami's removal, many analysts consider it unlikely that he will face serious consequences. He possesses sensitive operational knowledge regarding Venezuela's ties to Iran, Hezbollah, and covert state infrastructure. His fall from grace, therefore, is more indicative of power realignments within Chavismo than genuine accountability.

A Multi-Layered Network of Control and Chaos

The Chavista regime has developed a layered architecture of political, terrorist, and criminal operatives. This transregional apparatus advances a hybrid war model designed to destabilize democratic systems, infiltrate institutions, and suppress dissent through fear and strategic violence.

Key components of this network include:

1. Political Operative Cells

Tasked with exporting the Chavista ideology, these cells infiltrate civil society, influence political systems, and manipulate public discourse. Their objective is to undermine liberal democratic institutions and co-opt state structures through strategic alliances and proxy actors.

2. Violence and Intimidation Units

These specialized operatives are trained to instigate riots, harass opposition figures, and enforce compliance through fear. They benefit from legal impunity and are often embedded within local enforcement bodies or paramilitary collectives.

3. Terrorist Cells

Trained by Hezbollah and Quds Force operatives, these cells operate within Venezuela and across Latin America. They are equipped to execute destabilization campaigns, targeted assassinations, and symbolic acts of terror, with the ultimate aim of eroding state sovereignty and expanding ideological influence.

4. Financial Support Infrastructure

Through a complex web of money laundering, front companies, and crypto operations, the regime finances not only its survival but its external offensive. Funds derived from illicit narcotics, gold smuggling, and corruption are redirected into political campaigns, terror activities, and diplomatic subversion.

5. Paramilitary and Intelligence Hit Squads

These groups conduct abductions, torture, and targeted assassinations, particularly against dissidents, defectors, and external critics. Their operations are brutal, surgical, and insulated by state intelligence agencies such as DGCIM and SEBIN.

Conclusion: A Coordinated Front Against a Multi-Headed Threat

The Chavista regime's fusion of state power, terrorism, and criminal enterprise has created a strategic menace to the Western Hemisphere. The activities orchestrated from Venezuela, and projected across the Triple Frontier, represent a new paradigm of conflict — one that blurs the lines between war, crime, ideology, and politics.

Combating this threat requires more than sanctions or border patrols. It demands a comprehensive hemispheric doctrine of defense, involving intelligence fusion, institutional reform, multilateral coordination, and diplomatic isolation of narco-terrorist states.

If the nations of the Americas fail to recognize the symbiotic alliance between rogue regimes, terrorist proxies, and organized crime, the region risks succumbing to a long-term decay of democracy, sovereignty, and public security.

The Regional Hunt for the Enemies of the Narco-Terrorist Revolution: "Your House is My House – Su Casa es mi Casa"

In a climate of mounting domestic instability and eroding international legitimacy, the Maduro regime has resorted to increasingly desperate and repressive tactics. Masked behind so-called dialogues and negotiations—such as those held in Barbados in 2019 to address oil sanctions and electoral conditions—the regime has continued to entrench its power by manipulating legal mechanisms, reversing disqualifications at will, and disenfranchising legitimate opposition candidates.

These negotiations, often framed as democratic gestures, have strategically benefited the ruling elite, sidelining credible political challengers and enabling obscure, regime-aligned figures to rise. In essence, these maneuvers were not concessions but tactical diversions, designed to maintain Chavista hegemony under the illusion of electoral normalcy.

The Weaponization of "Bolivarian Fury"

Faced with what it portrayed as escalating coup threats, Maduro activated a chilling campaign known as "La Furia Bolivariana" (Bolivarian Fury)—a state-coordinated plan of internal and cross-border repression. This campaign mobilizes political operatives, intelligence networks, paramilitary groups, and criminal gangs, both within Venezuela and across Latin America, to target perceived enemies of the Revolution.

This strategy includes:
- Arbitrary arrests
- Political assassinations
- Cross-border abductions
- Harassment and psychological warfare
- Infiltration of diaspora communities

In early 2023, after denouncing multiple alleged coup plots, Maduro called on the military high command to maintain "maximum vigilance" and to unleash the "Bolivarian fury" against all dissidents. His rhetoric signaled not only a refusal to relinquish power but a formalization of a doctrine of regional repression.

The Assassination of Lt. Ronald Ojeda in Chile

Perhaps the most shocking demonstration of this doctrine occurred in Santiago, Chile. On February 21, 2024, Lt. Ronald Ojeda, a former Venezuelan army officer and political prisoner living under refugee status, was abducted and later murdered by a transnational hit team.

- Ojeda, 32, was living with his wife and young son on the 14th floor of a high-rise apartment.
- At 3:10 AM, four individuals—one in the lobby and three in fake Chilean Investigative Police (PDI) uniforms—forcibly removed him in his underwear and disappeared him without a trace.
- Surveillance footage captured the operation, and the only arrest made was of a 17-year-old Venezuelan with links to El Tren de Aragua, the regime's most powerful criminal proxy.
- Days later, Ojeda's body was found encased in cement in a method mirroring previous executions carried out by the cartel in northern Chile.

Ojeda was not an ordinary refugee. In 2017, after spending 239 days imprisoned in Ramo Verde, he escaped along with nine other officers. He was outspoken about his experience, posting messages of resistance and hope to other political prisoners. His assassination on foreign soil reveals the terrifying reach of Maduro's transnational repression apparatus.

Lt. Col. Alexander Granko: The Shadow Commander

The mastermind behind this and other transnational operations is Lt. Col. Alexander Granko, known as "Mano Negra" (Black Hand) and "The Man of a Thousand Faces". Granko, an elite military intelligence officer within DGCIM, is the chief architect of the Chavista regime's counterintelligence and regional sabotage strategy.

His operations extend beyond Venezuela's borders into:
- Colombia: where defectors and exiles have been harassed and targeted;

- Peru and Ecuador: where surveillance cells have been embedded in diaspora communities;
- Chile and Argentina: where coordinated campaigns of infiltration and disruption are being deployed;
- Spain and Mexico: where diplomatic cover is used to shield intelligence agents and criminal collaborators.

Granko's operations are cloaked in criminal anonymity but backed by state intelligence resources. He oversees cross-border kidnappings, assassinations, and the silencing of high-value dissidents, often in collaboration with narco-criminal partners and corrupt officials in host countries.

State Terror Without Borders

The Maduro regime's deployment of transnational repression through hybrid warfare tactics marks a new phase of geopolitical aggression in the Americas. It is no longer sufficient to view Venezuela as an internal humanitarian crisis; it must be recognized as the command center of a regional narco-terrorist campaign.
- The murder of Lt. Ronald Ojeda is not an isolated incident but a signal.
- The mobilization of "Bolivarian Fury" is not mere rhetoric but doctrine.
- The use of El Tren de Aragua and Granko's intelligence teams reveals a sophisticated infrastructure of extraterritorial terror.

This apparatus is designed to instill fear, deter defection, and export repression, all under the guise of defending a revolution that has long since morphed into an authoritarian criminal empire.

Addressing this threat requires:
- A joint hemispheric intelligence and protection initiative for exiled political dissidents;
- The designation of El Tren de Aragua and DGCIM as transnational criminal and terrorist entities;

- The formation of an inter-governmental task force on regional repression and cross-border criminality;
- And most urgently, a recognition by democratic nations that "your house is now their house"—and that no nation is safe if Venezuela's criminal state is allowed to operate with impunity.

The Transnational Intelligence War: DGCIM, ELN, and the Targeting of Venezuelan Dissidents in Colombia and Beyond

The export of Venezuela's repressive apparatus has reached an alarming level of sophistication. Coordinated operations involving the Directorate General of Military Counterintelligence (DGCIM), the ELN, and the Train of Aragua are now being documented across multiple Latin American countries, with Colombia as a principal theatre of operations.

These alliances form part of a broader strategy of regional counterinsurgency and persecution, in which criminal organizations are weaponized to track, surveil, intimidate, and eliminate Venezuelan dissidents residing abroad.

A Shadow Network of Kidnapping and Intelligence: The Case of Captain Ányelo Heredia and Others

In Colombia, intelligence operations directed from Caracas targeted high-profile dissidents such as:
- Captain Ányelo Heredia, a former military officer
- Lieutenant Ronald Ojeda, also a former officer and asylum seeker
- Pablo Parada, a student leader and political prisoner

According to exclusive reports by El Colombiano and Noticias Caracol (March–April 2024), these individuals were victims of a coordinated network involving criminal syndicates and regime intelligence operatives.

Captain Heredia was abducted in December 2023 in Norte de Santander, allegedly by ELN operatives who later handed him over to DGCIM agents. Heredia had warned in 2022 that his life was in danger following Gustavo Petro's presidential victory, stating that a shift in Colombian intelligence leadership would likely lead to his capture or extradition.

Lt. Ronald Ojeda, who was with Heredia near the Venezuelan border at the time, managed to escape by land—crossing through Ecuador and Peru before reaching Chile, where he later obtained refugee status. Tragically, despite his efforts, Ojeda was ultimately tracked and assassinated in Santiago, a case widely attributed to Venezuelan state-sponsored operatives acting through criminal proxies.

These events are not isolated incidents, but components of a systematic transnational hunt for regime dissidents.

A Testimony of Betrayal and Entrapment

As per Noticias Caracol, a former military contact testified:

"Captain Heredia contacted me. He told me about a mission—'Plan Free Venezuela'—that involved taking over the Táchira State, including a jungle battalion. I reviewed the operational plans, and something felt off. It was too polished. I warned them: 'If you want to cross into Venezuela, pretend to be vendors. Blend in. Don't use the trochas. But they didn't listen.'"

That warning proved prescient. Heredia was abducted. Ojeda fled. The operation they were drawn into was, most likely, a counterintelligence trap designed to lure deserters back across the border and deliver them to the regime's torturers.

The Ongoing Danger to Student Leader Pablo Parada

Another high-profile target, Pablo Parada, remains under extreme risk. Arrested in 2020 and subjected to severe physical and psychological torture, Parada has become a symbol of the regime's brutal approach to dissent.

His testimony is harrowing:

"They hung me from a tube with my hands cuffed, just my toes touching the floor. I was shocked in my genitals, had my toenails pulled out, was hung upside down, drowned in a water tank, strapped to a stretcher, covered in cloth, and subjected to simulated drowning. There's more, but it's too painful to recall."

Parada, like many others, is considered a traitor to the state simply for opposing Chavismo, making him a permanent target of its extraterritorial operations.

State-Sponsored Terror Without Borders

This section of the hemisphere has now become a warzone of intelligence and hybrid operations, in which:
- The Venezuelan state outsources repression to criminal organizations;
- Colombian territory is used as a hunting ground for dissidents and deserters;
- Transnational escape routes are compromised by surveillance and betrayal;
- And torture is systematically applied as both punishment and deterrence.

These developments are not only violations of human rights; they represent a direct threat to the sovereignty and security of host nations.

A Call for Regional Protection Protocols

The cases of Heredia, Ojeda, and Parada are emblematic of a much larger phenomenon: a narco-terrorist regime deploying counterintelligence warfare beyond its borders, with the assistance of criminal proxies and weak regional oversight.

To protect Venezuelan exiles, political prisoners, and military deserters, the following must be urgently addressed:

1. International protocols for the protection of political dissidents in exile, especially in Latin America;

2. Intelligence-sharing mechanisms between host nations to identify and prevent targeted abductions;

3. Criminal designation of the DGCIM, Train of Aragua, and their operatives as transnational actors engaged in state-sponsored terrorism;

4. Legal and diplomatic action against Maduro regime officials responsible for extraterritorial crimes.

The evidence is clear. The Venezuelan regime has turned intelligence into a weapon of exile warfare. Those who fled with hope are now hunted with impunity.

Hunting, Assassination, Abduction, and Pursuit. The Maduro Regime's Targeting of Opposition Figures in Colombia and Chile

Unveiling the Operations of Regional Terrorism and Criminal Networks

In late 2023, a dramatic and deeply concerning series of events began to unfold in Colombia and Chile, exposing a transnational campaign of political persecution orchestrated by the Maduro regime. This operation—a hybrid blend of state-sponsored terrorism, criminal outsourcing, and intelligence warfare—has targeted former Venezuelan military officers and civilian dissidents across Latin America.

An alleged plot to overthrow Nicolás Maduro was used as a pretext for a ruthless campaign of transnational reprisals. According to a multi-part investigative report by Noticias Caracol, the regime's intelligence apparatus acted in coordination with powerful criminal groups—specifically the ELN and the Train of Aragua—to hunt down individuals identified as conspirators. This campaign has blatantly violated the sovereignty of host nations and revealed the deep operational reach of Venezuela's intelligence services.

The Meeting in Cúcuta: The Spark that Lit the Fuse

On December 13, 2023, a group of Venezuelan military deserters gathered in a modest residence in a residential neighborhood of Cúcuta, Colombia. Devoid of weapons, funding, or institutional support, their aim was symbolic—a final attempt to organize a movement to liberate Venezuela. This clandestine meeting would later be used by the regime as justification for launching a regional manhunt.

Unbeknownst to the attendees, the regime already had knowledge of the meeting, likely through infiltrated informants or surveillance technology. Within days, events would unfold that confirmed the worst fears of Venezuela's exiled opposition: that no border could protect them, and that the regime had both the means and the will to pursue them across sovereign territories.

A source who attended the meeting and later spoke to Noticias Caracol under condition of anonymity recounted:

"Captain Heredia contacted me, told me I had a mission, and that we would meet in Norte de Santander. I was shown a plan—an operation called 'Free Venezuela'—which involved taking over the Táchira State, the Army brigade, and the 21st jungle infantry battalion. But something didn't feel right. I saw the military planning table. I saw all the operational schematics. And I said—no, something here is off."

In hindsight, what they were seeing may have been a counterintelligence trap designed by the DGCIM itself.

The Targets: Heredia, Ojeda, and Parada

Three individuals have emerged as key victims of this transnational operation:

1. Captain Ányelo Heredia – a former Venezuelan officer who had previously fled to Colombia and attempted to reach the United States via the treacherous Darién Gap. After returning to Colombia for the meeting in Cúcuta, he was kidnapped by ELN operatives near the border and handed over to the DGCIM.

2. Lieutenant Ronald Ojeda – another former officer and escapee from Venezuelan military prison, Ojeda had fled by land through Ecuador and Peru before securing asylum in Chile. In February 2024, he was abducted from his apartment in Santiago by criminals impersonating Chilean police, later identified as members of the Train of Aragua acting under direction from Venezuelan intelligence. His body was found buried in cement, a hallmark of the regime's extraterritorial executions.

3. Pablo Parada – a student leader, opposition figure, and survivor of Venezuelan prison torture, Parada was recently attacked in Bogotá by an armed criminal group allegedly acting as enforcers for the regime's transnational repression network.

The Warnings, the Disregard, and the Consequences

According to testimonies from former comrades-in-arms, Captain Heredia and Lt. Ojeda were warned not to cross into Venezuela through illicit routes. A fellow soldier told Noticias Caracol:

"I told them, 'Don't do it. If you're going to cross, blend in. Dress like vendors, wear sandals, act like poor people. But they didn't listen. They chose the illegal path and were ambushed.'"

Indeed, the border region of Norte de Santander—a zone already known for cartel trafficking and guerrilla activity—became the trap. Captain Heredia was intercepted by members of the ELN, who reportedly had standing arrangements with the DGCIM, and was forcibly transferred to Venezuelan authorities.

Lt. Ojeda, more cautious, escaped. But even in exile, he was not safe. Months later, the Train of Aragua tracked him down in Santiago, Chile, and executed a military-style abduction at 3:10 a.m., impersonating Chilean Investigative Police (PDI). Despite the brutality of the kidnapping—he was dragged away in underwear—there was no ransom. The event was political, not economic.

His corpse was later discovered encased in concrete in a northern Chilean construction site. The message was clear: the regime has reach—and it has no mercy.

The Weaponization of Criminal Networks for Political Elimination

This episode underscores the new face of Venezuelan repression: one that merges intelligence services, proxy criminal networks, and foreign territory to pursue regime enemies.

What is unfolding is not merely political persecution. It is state-directed international terrorism. And it reflects a larger truth: the Venezuelan regime is no longer confined to its borders—it is projecting violence across the hemisphere.

The regional and international community must urgently recognize this new reality and take coordinated action to:
• Protect exiled dissidents and political refugees from transnational persecution;
• Identify and sanction officials within the DGCIM, ELN, and Train of Aragua involved in cross-border operations;
• Strengthen asylum safeguards for at-risk individuals from Venezuela;
• And establish accountability mechanisms to prevent the normalization of political assassinations on foreign soil.

These events are not isolated. They are part of a pattern. And the silence of institutions only emboldens the perpetrators.

Torture as State Doctrine: The Case of Pablo Parada

A Survivor's Testimony in the Age of Transnational Repression

While Captain Heredia and Lieutenant Ojeda became emblematic victims of a cross-border manhunt, a third name emerges with haunting resonance: Pablo Parada, a student leader, political dissident, and survivor of the Maduro regime's torture machinery.

In 2020, Parada was arrested in Venezuela after participating in civic demonstrations and actively denouncing the regime's authoritarian consolidation. What followed was not a judicial process—but a descent into state-sanctioned hell.

Parada's own words, later shared publicly, offer a window into a systematic torture apparatus designed not only to extract confessions but to break the human spirit:

"When they captured me, they hung me by my wrists, handcuffed to a high metal bar, leaving only the tips of my toes touching the floor—for hours. I received electric shocks to my genitals. They ripped out parts of my toenails. They hung me upside down and submerged my head repeatedly in a water tank. They laid me on a stretcher, placed a cloth over my face, and poured water to simulate drowning. I could go on... but there are things too painful to remember."

These practices are not anecdotal. They reflect institutionalized torture protocols within the General Directorate of Military Counterintelligence (DGCIM) and the Bolivarian National Intelligence Service (SEBIN), documented by international human rights bodies and corroborated by dozens of survivors. Torture has become a tactical instrument of fear, used to dismantle resistance and enforce ideological submission.

Parada survived. But his scars are permanent—both physical and psychological. His case underscores a terrifying truth: the Venezuelan regime has normalized torture as a method of governance.

After escaping to Colombia, Parada attempted to rebuild his life and continue his activism. But even in exile, the threat followed him. In early 2024, he was attacked in Bogotá by a criminal cell linked—according to regional intelligence sources—to networks affiliated with the Train of Aragua, acting as external enforcers of the Chavista counterintelligence complex.

His case remains under investigation. But one fact is undisputed: Parada's life is at risk. And his story is not unique.

Systemic Repression, Transnational Machinery

Pablo Parada is one among many. His testimony is echoed by countless dissidents, activists, and former officials who have fled Venezuela only to find that the reach of repression is not bounded by geography. From Santiago to Bogotá, from Cúcuta to Miami, the Maduro regime is operating an extraterritorial system of persecution—backed by criminal alliances, enabled by state intelligence, and shielded by the impunity of international silence.

These operations are not rogue. They are doctrinal.

They reflect the mutation of Venezuela from a failed democracy into a criminal state prototype, where the instruments of national security are weaponized against the population—and then exported abroad.

The evidence is mounting. And the international community must no longer avert its gaze.

Venezuela's Transnational Criminal-Terrorist Network: A Strategic Hemispheric Threat

After years of silent expansion, what once seemed a disjointed collection of ideological allies and exiled revolutionaries has crystallized into a continental architecture of repression, terrorism, and criminal coordination. This Venezuelan Transnational Network, rooted in the doctrines of Chavismo and hybrid warfare, now constitutes one of the most potent asymmetric threats to democratic stability in the Western Hemisphere.

1. The Paradigm: State Intelligence as the Engine of Revolution

At the core of this architecture are the Venezuelan intelligence and counterintelligence agencies, notably:
- DGCIM (Dirección General de Contrainteligencia Militar)
- SEBIN (Servicio Bolivariano de Inteligencia Nacional)

These two entities operate not simply as internal repressive arms but as exporters of terror and control, tasked with identifying, monitoring, infiltrating, and neutralizing dissidents and threats — both domestic and foreign.

Their operations increasingly depend on irregular alliances with:
- The ELN (Ejército de Liberación Nacional)
- The Tren de Aragua
- Released criminal operatives loyal to the regime
- Hezbollah operatives embedded in Latin America

These agents act through clandestine intelligence posts embedded within sympathetic or weak host countries.

2. Strategic Structure of the Operational Network

This hemispheric model, established since 2006 and perfected through the collapse of institutional resistance, is structured around four core command nodes and their affiliated functions:

Iran – Strategic Direction and Training
- Leads ideological indoctrination rooted in Islamic fundamentalism.
- Trains Latin American recruits (including Venezuelans) in:
- Urban terrorism
- Explosives and weapons

- Clandestine operations
- Coordinates deployments with its proxies, notably Hezbollah and Quds Force.

Venezuela – Hemispheric Command Center
- Operational hub for strategy and coordination.
- Recruitment and radicalization of Venezuelan youth and Latin American dissidents.
- Actors:
- DGCIM
- SEBIN
- Quds Force
- Hezbollah
- Cartel del Sol
- ELN
- ISIS cells
- Cartel de Sinaloa (as logistical and narcotics enabler)

Cuba – Intelligence and Political Subversion
- Through its G2 intelligence service, Cuba:
- Trains Chavista and Latin American cadres in political indoctrination.
- Provides field operatives and logistical support.
- Infiltrates institutions via diplomatic and cultural fronts.

Nicaragua – Communications and Logistics Hub
- Offers intelligence coordination spaces.
- Facilitates secure regional communications.
- Hosts revolutionary coordination platforms under state protection.

3. Infrastructure of Infiltration and Action

These networks are embedded across the continent through a multilayered architecture of covert and semi-covert operations, including:
- Cultural Centers (used for soft power and recruitment)
- Religious Centers (used by Iranian-affiliated clerics and Hezbollah operatives)

- Indoctrination Centers (often disguised as educational exchanges)
- Training Bases (secret, militarized, and embedded in jungle or rural zones)
- Coordination Cells (political agents influencing elections and media)
- Violent Action Bases (to activate street violence during political crises)
- Special Operations Cells (for targeted killings, kidnappings, and intimidation)

Each structure includes a command nucleus:
- Trained military or intelligence operatives
- Embedded political agents
- Former prisoners or loyalist criminals
- Foreign operatives from Iran, Hezbollah, and others

4. Regional Penetration and Proxy Warfare

The regime's influence does not end at borders. Through these transnational bases, the Maduro regime has:

- Infiltrated opposition communities abroad to monitor and neutralize dissent.
- Supported political and criminal factions in host countries, leveraging shared interests in anti-Western, anti-democratic objectives.
- Secured alliances with permissive or corrupt governments, particularly in Bolivia, Nicaragua, and segments of Brazil and Argentina.
- Enabled the laundering of illicit revenues (oil, drugs, gold) through shell institutions and sanctioned-exempt trade routes.

This amounts to a non-traditional theater of war, where ideological warfare, narcotrafficking, and political sabotage converge.

5. The Iran–Venezuela–Hezbollah Axis: A Strategic Deepening

Since 2006, Iran has used Venezuela as a launchpad for hemispheric projection, leveraging oil-for-intelligence exchanges, technological partnerships, and cultural influence. This alliance, though informal in appearance, is strategic in essence:

- Hezbollah has established strongholds in Paraguay, Argentina, Venezuela, Colombia, and Brazil.
- Venezuela has issued false documentation and passports to Hezbollah operatives.
- Iranian-Quds aligned operatives train paramilitary cells in the Andes and Caribbean.
- Joint ventures in mining, energy, and port access have offered a disguise for weapons smuggling and financial laundering.

6. A Threat to Regional Sovereignty and Security

This network has allowed the Maduro regime — now fused with narco-terrorist logic — to:
- Project intimidation across borders
- Eliminate opponents in exile (as with Ronald Ojeda)
- Destabilize host countries
- Undermine democracies from within

It is not merely a Venezuelan issue — it is a continental threat.

Conclusion of Section

What we face is not a traditional dictatorship or isolated regime. It is a transnational criminal-terrorist consortium that has weaponized ideology, intelligence, and illicit capital to embed itself within the institutional veins of the Americas. Disrupting this structure will require not only sanctions and condemnations but the formation of a counter-network of intelligence coordination, legal accountability, and civil society resilience across the hemisphere.

The Chavista–Iranian–Hezbollah Network in Latin America

Since 2006, the Chavista regime has orchestrated the establishment of a continental network of revolutionary, criminal, and terrorist cells that now spans nearly every country in Latin America. This structure is strategically differentiated by national geopolitical interest and composed of several key operational bases:

• Iran: Leads ideological indoctrination and paramilitary training, hosting activists and students from across Latin America. Training areas include urban terrorism, explosives, and weapons handling.

• Venezuela: Functions as the hemispheric strategic hub, coordinating operations through the DGCIM, SEBIN, Quds Force, Hezbollah, FARC, ELN, the Cartel of the Suns, Sinaloa Cartel, and others.

• Cuba: Provides seasoned political operatives and intelligence support via the G2 service.

• Nicaragua: Facilitates communication and logistical support.

These bases—whether embedded in cultural or religious centers, political offices, or clandestine training sites—serve multiple purposes: ideological indoctrination, regional coordination, covert operations, and violent mobilization. Many also operate as hubs for transnational crime, espionage, and recruitment.

Hezbollah, empowered by Iran, has expanded its presence across Argentina, Brazil, Paraguay, and Colombia through illicit financing operations such as drug trafficking and money laundering. Venezuela provides these actors with a safe haven, state support, forged documentation, and operational freedom.

The Chavista regime further enables criminal actors, former convicts, and radical militants to operate freely—serving as enforcers and subversive agents across host nations. Their role extends beyond violence to include manipulating public opinion, lobbying institutions, and orchestrating grassroots agitation.

Parallel to this, the growing alliance between Iran and Bolivia, revived under President Luis Arce, has triggered regional concern. Their cooperation—now extending into security, defense, drone deployment, and military training—mirrors the Venezuelan model. Analysts warn that these agreements lack legitimate bilateral rationale and instead function as platforms for ideological and operational infiltration.

Scholars such as Paulo Botta and official reports by the U.S. State Department have confirmed Hezbollah's operational footprint in Latin America, including fundraising and logistical activities in Brazil, Chile, Colombia, Panama, Peru, and the United States.

Strategic Conclusion

The convergence of the Chavista regime, Iran, and Hezbollah constitutes a transnational axis of authoritarianism, criminality, and terrorism. Their collective aim is to erode democratic governance, destabilize regional security, and expand geopolitical influence through clandestine operations, ideological penetration, and hybrid warfare.

Confronting this threat demands:

- Robust regional cooperation in intelligence sharing, law enforcement, and judicial response.
- Targeted sanctions against state and non-state enablers of terrorist financing and facilitation.
- Strengthening democratic institutions, civil society, and economic opportunity to undercut the recruitment base for extremist networks.

This evolving network is not merely a geopolitical anomaly—it is a strategic and ongoing assault on sovereignty, democracy, and hemispheric stability.

Seeds of Suspicion — Narco-terrorism, Regional Reach, and U.S. Designations

Conclusion: From Genesis to Global Narco-terror Threat

The narco-terrorist state that took root under Chavismo was neither accidental nor chaotic—it was the result of a carefully cultivated convergence of criminal trafficking, extremist ideology, and authoritarian governance. Venezuela's strategic geography, coupled with systemic corruption in its armed forces and judicial institutions, enabled it to become the central node of a hemispheric web of terror and illicit commerce.

Narco-terrorist Networks and State Complicity

What began as facilitation of FARC and ELN coca shipments in the early 2000s evolved into full state authorization of transnational criminal operations. Under Chavez, and increasingly under Maduro, Venezuelan military and intelligence services (DGCIM, SEBIN) became instrumental in sustaining the Cartel de los Soles—an entity composed of senior Venezuelan officials and criminal actors. This network extended its reach to Hezbollah, Iran, the Sinaloa Cartel, ISIS-linked agents, and leftist armed groups across continental Latin America.

These transnational connections functioned through cultural centers, secret indoctrination and training camps, local coordination cells, and street action groups. Beyond Venezuelan borders—in countries like Colombia, Argentina, Brazil, Bolivia, Mexico, Panama, and others—oil wealth, political operatives, and clandestine infrastructure were leveraged for both ideological influence and operational mobilization.

The U.S. Response: Designating the Cartel de los Soles as a Terrorist Entity

As of July 25, 2025, the U.S. Department of the Treasury officially designated the Cartel de los Soles as a Specially Designated Global Terrorist (SDGT) organization. In tandem, the State Department named it a Foreign Terrorist Organization (FTO) due to its support for already designated terror groups like the Tren de Aragua and the Sinaloa Cartel .

Secretary Bessent stated these steps "expose the illegitimate Maduro regime's facilitation of narco-terrorism." These designations extend U.S. sanctions and penalties to Maduro and other high-ranking officials tied to the Cartel's operations .

This marks one of the first times in U.S. history that an institutionalized, government-linked cartel has been formally classified as a terrorist threat, blurring the lines between traditional criminal syndicates and ideological terrorism .

Why This Matters: A Turning Point in Global Security

• Legal and financial consequences: These U.S. designations open the door for far-reaching sanctions, asset seizures, and global cooperation to dismantle financial and operational structures tied to narco-terrorism.

• A shift in narrative and policy: Labeling Cartel de los Soles as a global terror entity reframes Venezuela not as a failing state in crisis, but as a deliberate, state-sponsored narco-terrorist regime.

• Regional wake-up call: The hemispheric expansion of Chavista criminal-terror networks—including networks in Colombia, Chile, Argentina, Brazil, and Mexico—cannot be ignored. This requires coordinated, multilateral responses across borders.

Transition to Chapter 5

In Chapter 5, we will delve into the profiles and operations of the Tren de Aragua, Cartel Sinaloa, and similar FTO-designated groups intertwined with the Venezuelan regime. We will map out the operational partnerships, financing routes, and ideological indoctrination programs that underpin this narco-terror state's reach. The focus will be on the structure, reach, and ideological cohesion of this global menace—and the strategies necessary to counter it.

Chapter 5
CROSSING BORDERS: How the Chavista Narco-Terror Revolution Reached American Soil

The Ominous Chill: The Narco-Terror's Shadow Over America

"The Ominous Chill: The Narco-Terror's Shadow Over America"
"But where darkness spreads,
a light will rise.

For in the face of tyranny,
they rise.
They resist.

Shadows creep across the borders,
whispers of narco-terror seep through the cracks.

The Chavista revolution advances—dark, deliberate, bold—
its tendrils reaching far, sowing silence and fear.

From distant lands it infiltrates,
piercing the heart of America,
leaving chaos in its wake
and doubt in the minds of the free.

Hidden channels carry its poison.
Uncertainty echoes through halls of power.
Once sovereign and still, American soil
now trembles beneath an ominous chill.

But where darkness spreads,
a light will rise.
Brave souls draw a line in the sand,
unshaken in the silence of the night.

Across borders, the struggle unfolds—

yet liberty's spirit endures.

In the face of tyranny,

they rise.

They resist.

And they defend the sacred ground they call home.

— Johan Obdola

Chavismo's Shadow on American Soil: Infiltration, Radicalization, and Criminal Expansion

The growing presence of Chavismo and its terrorist and criminal affiliates within the United States represents a complex and underrecognized threat to national security and democratic integrity. Despite the United States' longstanding role as a bulwark against authoritarian regimes, extremist networks, and narco-terrorism, new fault lines have emerged—allowing agents of Venezuela's revolutionary state, and its allies, to quietly penetrate and destabilize from within.

This infiltration is neither abstract nor incidental. It is strategic, transnational, and increasingly visible in key corridors of influence, criminal activity, and ideological subversion.

Strategic Infiltration of Institutions and Influence Networks

One of the primary mechanisms through which Chavismo has extended its reach is via the infiltration of Venezuelan embassies, consulates, and affiliated diplomatic missions in the U.S. These structures—once intended for consular service—have in many instances become platforms for soft-power projection, regime propaganda, and political interference. Within their networks operate lobbying groups, activist fronts, and think tanks aligned with the Bolivarian cause. Often masked under humanitarian, cultural, or academic programs, these actors promote disinformation, foster ideological sympathy, and identify potential collaborators.

Sympathetic officials within these nodes have reportedly facilitated covert meetings, financial transfers, and legal protections for operatives tied to the Venezuelan state. These efforts are not isolated—they form part of a coordinated strategy of geopolitical disruption and hemispheric penetration.

Convergence of Terror and Crime

The threat posed by Chavismo-aligned networks on U.S. soil is further amplified by their convergence with terrorist and criminal entities. Elements associated with Hezbollah and the Islamic State have been linked to support or sanctuary networks connected to the Venezuelan regime and its diaspora. This includes the reported presence of over 600 Latin Americans recruited by ISIS—many of whom returned to Latin America and are suspected of moving transnationally.

At the same time, the presence of violent gangs such as El Tren de Aragua—a Venezuelan-origin cartel with deep ties to the Maduro regime—is now confirmed in multiple U.S. jurisdictions. This criminal group, acting as an operational extension of Chavismo's narco-state, engages in trafficking, extortion, and targeted violence, and has become one of the fastest-growing transnational criminal threats in the Western Hemisphere.

The regime's fusion of political ideology with organized crime and terrorism has evolved into a hybrid threat model—one that exports destabilization while disguising it as migration, diplomacy, or ideological resistance.

Illicit Activities and Domestic Destabilization

Chavismo's operational presence also manifests in a spectrum of illicit activities conducted on American soil. These include:
- Money laundering operations facilitated through shell companies and cryptocurrency channels.
- Drug trafficking and arms smuggling with logistical support from transnational partners.
- Cyber operations and financial fraud targeting U.S. institutions and vulnerable populations.
- Human trafficking and coercive networks, often operating through migrant corridors and border vulnerabilities.

These networks not only undermine U.S. law enforcement capacity but also erode institutional trust and public safety across multiple states.

Recruitment and Ideological Radicalization

Perhaps more insidious than physical infiltration is the ideological campaign underway within diaspora communities and politically vulnerable sectors. Chavismo and its aligned operatives have launched coordinated recruitment and radicalization efforts, particularly targeting disenfranchised Latin American youth and refugee populations. These campaigns often deploy narratives of resistance, anti-imperialism, and economic justice—weaponizing legitimate grievances to manufacture loyalty to a criminal regime.

The presence of these networks in American academic spaces, cultural events, and political demonstrations demands urgent scrutiny. What appears as civic expression may in fact be a front for recruitment and surveillance operations linked to the broader revolutionary objective.

Challenges to US Values and Interests: The expansion of Chavismo in the US represents a challenge to fundamental American values and interests. It undermines democratic principles, threatens national security, and contributes to regional instability. Moreover, it complicates US efforts to promote democracy and human rights in the Western Hemisphere, as Chavismo-aligned regimes seek to export their authoritarian model beyond Venezuela's borders.

The presence of Chavismo and its allies in the US presents a complex and evolving threat. It requires a comprehensive and coordinated response from law enforcement, intelligence agencies, policymakers, and civil society. Effectively addressing this threat will require vigilance, resilience, and a commitment to upholding democratic norms and the rule of law.

The Bolivarian Fury on American Soil

For over 15 years, the Venezuelan regime—under the strategic coordination of Iran, with operational support from Cuba and Nicaragua—has exploited the rising waves of mass migration from Latin America as a deliberate mechanism to infiltrate the United States and, to a lesser extent, Canada. Within these forced displacements, criminal elements, trained operatives, and ideological radicals have moved undetected, blurring the line between refugee and infiltrator. This migration dynamic has become a powerful tool for asymmetric warfare, carefully designed and deployed by what can only be described as a transnational narco-terrorist axis.

Far from being spontaneous, this process is embedded within a larger geopolitical strategy. It leverages humanitarian crises, weaponizes displacement, and injects agents into the heart of Western democracies. The objective is clear: destabilize from within.

An Expanding Geopolitical Storm

The convergence of regional collapse and global confrontation is rapidly transforming the security architecture of the Americas. The toxic blend of economic recession, weakened democratic institutions, and rising authoritarian populism across Latin America and the Caribbean has created fertile ground for the Chavista regime and its allies to execute a hemispheric insurgency.

This insurgency is not isolated. It is connected—deliberately and operationally—to broader global tensions:
- The Israel–Hamas war, reigniting radical fervor.
- Russia's aggression in Ukraine, normalizing hybrid warfare and disinformation at scale.
- Iran's ideological and strategic push against Israel and the West.
- China's cyber warfare and regional expansionism, particularly against Taiwan and in the South China Sea.
- The resurgence of ISIS and jihadist groups, including renewed threats via encrypted social media and deep web channels.

These overlapping crises indicate more than coincidence. They form a loose but converging axis of authoritarian and extremist forces, each advancing its agenda—political, ideological, or territorial—through hybrid and asymmetric methods. If these forces coordinate—or even overlap in timing—the result could be a multi-front crisis capable of plunging global societies into fear, paralysis, and collapse.

Latin America's Migrant Corridor: A Trojan Horse

Within this matrix, the migrant waves entering the United States have tragically become a literal gateway for radicalized actors, embedded operatives, and criminal enforcers. While the majority of migrants are victims fleeing poverty and repression, intelligence reports and field data confirm that terrorist sympathizers, Iranian proxy operatives, Hezbollah agents, and members of Venezuela's armed criminal groups have exploited these routes.

At the center of this infiltration is a doctrine I have identified as the "Bolivarian Fury Against the Empire"—a long-term, low-visibility campaign aimed at weakening the United States from within. These operatives are not idle. Their objectives are tactical and clear:

• Facilitate illicit operations such as money laundering, weapons and drug smuggling, and underground financial flows.

• Recruit and radicalize vulnerable Latin American youth, including second-generation migrants in U.S. communities.

• Establish operational cells capable of creating chaos during targeted disruption events—potentially leading to terrorist acts or destabilizing incidents at moments of national vulnerability.

These actions are not isolated gestures of dissent. They are structured, financed, and activated—ultimately responding to command-and-control nodes located in Tehran and Caracas.

U.S. Response: A New Phase of Confrontation

Under the second presidential term of Donald J. Trump, a more aggressive posture has been adopted in direct response to these threats. Two measures stand out as unprecedented and strategically significant:

1. The designation of the Venezuelan regime's Cartel de los Soles as a foreign terrorist organization, formally recognizing its role as a global criminal entity with ties to drug trafficking, terrorism, and international destabilization.

2. The initiation of mass deportation operations targeting members of El Tren de Aragua—a hyper-violent Venezuelan criminal organization with operational nodes in multiple U.S. states. These efforts mark a critical pivot in U.S. domestic counterterrorism, elevating Venezuela-linked transnational crime to a national security priority.

These developments signal a shift from observation to confrontation. Yet, the threat remains active and decentralized. While Washington begins to act, the networks seeded over more than a decade continue to operate—awaiting new directives, new opportunities, or the fateful arrival of what some in these radical circles call "Day Zero."

Structures of the Bolivarian Fury and Its Proxies in the United States

The asymmetric infiltration of the United States by the Chavista regime and its radical allies is neither spontaneous nor isolated. It is part of a meticulously coordinated effort—what I have termed the "Bolivarian Fury"—to undermine democratic institutions, propagate ideological subversion, and facilitate transnational criminal operations.

Over the course of years of investigation and collaboration with security experts and intelligence specialists across the Americas, I have identified five distinct operational structures currently deployed on American soil. Each serves a critical function within a broader hemispheric strategy directed from Caracas, Havana, Tehran, and beyond.

1. Intelligence Agents and Coordinators

At the core of this architecture are embedded operatives belonging to Venezuela's intelligence apparatus:
- DGCIM (Directorate General of Military Counterintelligence)
- SEBIN (Bolivarian Intelligence Service)
- Quds Force advisors (operating under Iranian coordination)
- Cuban intelligence handlers

These agents are responsible for:
- Receiving encrypted communications and strategic directives.
- Coordinating field operations across different regions of the U.S.
- Managing clandestine logistics for operatives and sleeper cells.
- Shielding key assets under diplomatic or informal cover.

Their operational cells often remain dormant until activated—serving both as facilitators and enforcers within the ecosystem of Chavista proxies abroad.

2. Electronic Intelligence and Cyber Operations Units

Cyber disruption is a key pillar in this unconventional campaign. The Bolivarian networks maintain cyber cells tasked with:
- Executing minor to mid-level cyberattacks on U.S. targets.
- Coordinating with allied cyberwarfare entities from Iran, China, Russia, Nicaragua, and Venezuela.
- Testing U.S. digital infrastructure vulnerabilities in coordination with foreign intelligence partners.
- Disseminating digital propaganda and disinformation across Spanish-speaking platforms.

These units contribute to the destabilization of public trust, institutional processes, and inter-agency coordination.

3. Political Mobilization and Radicalization Units

Chavismo's ideological penetration also relies on political operatives embedded in radical activism. This group includes:
- Trained youth from Cuba, Venezuela, and Iran.
- Sympathizers embedded in Latino community networks.

- Ultra-left groups sympathetic to Bolivarian ideology.
- Foreign-trained political agitators linked to "Bolivarian missions."

Their objectives include:
- Organizing protests, riots, and political disruptions.
- Influencing local elections and narratives within U.S. Hispanic communities.
- Promoting anti-U.S., anti-capitalist, and revolutionary propaganda.
- Operating under the cover of social justice movements or humanitarian aid.

4. Terrorist Agents and Extremist Operatives

Perhaps the most concerning layer involves direct operatives from global terrorist networks with ties to the Chavista regime:
- Hezbollah
- Quds Force
- ISIS returnees from Latin America
- FARC and ELN militants
- Minor radical groups from across Latin America

These operatives:
- Often possess Venezuelan or Nicaraguan passports for mobility.
- Operate in small, compartmentalized cells across U.S. urban centers.
- Are trained for paramilitary action, logistical support, or lone-wolf operations.
- Coordinate with or serve as proxies for Iranian-aligned intelligence operations.

Their presence signals a dangerous convergence of ideology, criminality, and terrorism.

5. Criminal Expansion and Street-Level Operatives

Two identifiable categories of criminal actors have established footholds on U.S. soil. The most prominent is El Tren de Aragua, now recognized as one of the most violent transnational criminal organizations born under Chavismo's protection.

El Tren de Aragua

- Originated in Tocorón Prison, Venezuela, under the eye of Tareck El Aissami and Nicolás Maduro.
- Initially used to suppress political protests and neutralize rival gangs within Venezuela.
- Rapidly expanded across Latin America, Spain, parts of Africa, and now the U.S., functioning like a narco-paramilitary franchise.
- Operates through extortion, contract killing, human trafficking, drug trafficking, and coercive territorial control.
- Comprised of brutal factions like "Los Gallegos", which publicly threaten communities abroad, including in Peru, Chile, and potentially U.S. cities.

As documented by Ojo Público, their modus operandi mimics terrorist insurgency—media intimidation, paramilitary symbolism, and violent public threats to communities perceived as hostile.

This gang exemplifies how the Chavista regime has fused criminal enterprise with ideological warfare, deploying crime not as a consequence, but as a weapon.

These five interconnected structures form a multilayered web of influence, infiltration, and violence, directed by hostile regimes and protected by institutional blind spots across the Western Hemisphere. Their operations, while not yet fully exposed, are escalating in sophistication and reach.

The presence of the Bolivarian Fury within the United States is not a projection—it is a reality, and it demands urgent strategic, institutional, and civic response.

The Rise of a Criminal Mega-Franchise: El Tren de Aragua's Transnational Expansion

As chilling videos of armed Venezuelan gangs circulated across South America—particularly in Peru, where factions of El Tren de Aragua publicly threatened entire districts—authorities in Ecuador announced the capture of one of the group's top leaders: Hernán David Landaeta, also known as José Manuel Vera Sulbarán or alias Satanás. His arrest symbolized not the fall of a criminal leader, but the exposure of a violent, rapidly expanding transnational crime franchise born under the Chavista regime.

Since approximately 2018, coinciding with the most intense waves of Venezuelan migration, El Tren de Aragua has left behind a brutal trail of extortion, human trafficking, assassinations, and territorial takeovers. From Colombia to Ecuador, Peru, and Chile, this hybrid criminal apparatus has not merely operated—it has displaced local gangs, taken control of key urban zones and border corridors, and established "plazas"—territorial domains where they exert de facto control.

This is no longer a Venezuelan problem. It is a continental crisis.

Investigative Intelligence: NarcoFiles and the Trail of Violence

Through NarcoFiles, an international investigative project coordinated by the Organized Crime and Corruption Reporting Project (OCCRP) and the Latin American Center for Investigative Journalism (CLIP), OjoPúblico gained access to a massive trove of leaked emails, classified police reports, and intelligence documents from Colombian military and security services (spanning 2019–2022).

Cross-referenced with street-level reporting, court documents, and interviews with police and victims, this investigation paints a staggering picture:
- Colombian authorities tracked the expansion of El Tren de Aragua and its armed factions from Venezuelan border zones into Colombia, Peru, and Ecuador.

• In areas such as Arauca and Norte de Santander, their forces often coexisted—and at times clashed—with Residual Organized Armed Groups (GAOR) and FARC/ELN dissidents.

• These groups, baptized as heirs to past insurgencies and drug cartels, now operate in a new ecosystem of narco-terrorist hybridization.

The Peru Front: Violence, Territory, and Lawlessness

The scope of El Tren de Aragua's operations in Peru alone is alarming:

• Between 2018 and 2023, Peruvian authorities recorded at least 219 arrests of individuals linked to the gang.

• Of these, 83.5% occurred in 2023, reflecting a sharp escalation.

• Hotspots of activity include urban districts of Lima Metropolitana (San Martín de Porres, Comas, Los Olivos, Santa Anita, Ate, etc.) as well as regional centers like La Libertad, Arequipa, Cusco, and Tacna.

This expansion strategy mirrors that of insurgent operations: entering soft zones, exploiting institutional weakness, and dominating through fear.

Origins of a Criminal State Prototype

The roots of El Tren de Aragua stretch back to the era of Hugo Chávez, between 2007 and 2010. Emerging from the workers' union of a government railway project in Aragua state, the group began by extorting local contractors and dominating the labor market. It quickly mutated—by 2013, following Chávez's death and under Governor Tareck El Aissami, the group secured protection, autonomy, and reach.

By turning Tocorón Prison into its operational hub, the group grew into a protected arm of state-sanctioned criminal enforcement, used to suppress protests and eliminate rivals. Maduro's regime gave it space to evolve as a proxy force, tasked with controlling local populations and expanding Venezuelan influence abroad.

2018: The Turning Point

The year 2018 marked a critical juncture. The Organization of American States (OAS) declared Venezuelan migration the "largest in the history of the Western Hemisphere." That same year, El Tren de Aragua began to embed itself in the Andean corridor, blending seamlessly with humanitarian migration waves.

- Colombia hosted 1 million Venezuelans, followed by Peru (395,000), Ecuador (250,000), and Chile (84,000).
- By 2023, these numbers more than doubled: 2.4 million in Colombia, over 1 million in Peru, and growing numbers elsewhere.
- Amid weakened governance due to the pandemic and economic downturns, El Tren de Aragua and other criminal groups seized control of migrant routes, border towns, and resource-rich urban corridors.

What began as a regional gang has now metastasized into an international criminal organism, deeply rooted in a state-sponsored ecosystem of violence, impunity, and ideological warfare.

"Niño Guerrero" and the Criminal Archetype of a Broken Nation

At the heart of the Tren de Aragua criminal expansion lies a man who, by all conventional metrics, should have been nothing more than a footnote in Venezuela's long list of petty criminals. Instead, Héctor Guerrero Flores, known as Niño Guerrero, rose to become one of the most notorious fugitives in Latin America—a brutal symbol of how a culture of impunity, mediocrity, and systemic corruption can manufacture its own criminal legends.

Arrested in 2010 at just 27 years old, Guerrero Flores was sentenced to 17 years in prison for homicide, drug trafficking, and weapons possession. Yet far from being neutralized, his imprisonment became the catalyst for his rise. From inside Tocorón Prison—a facility that would later become the nerve center of El Tren de Aragua—Guerrero began to consolidate control. He first escaped in 2012, was recaptured in 2013, and again became the self-declared Pran (a Venezuelan prison term meaning "Natural Born Killer – Supreme Inmate Authority").

Within Venezuela's collapsed penitentiary system, being a Pran means more than power—it means absolute control, complete autonomy, and open lines of communication with the outside world. By September 2023, Guerrero had escaped again. He remains at large to this day. The Peruvian government currently offers a reward of 132,000 USD for information leading to his capture.

Criminal Culture as Political Currency

The case of Niño Guerrero illustrates a deeper pathology: how a failed state transforms common delinquents into warlords, and how social decay breeds symbolic power for those who master violence. Guerrero—uneducated, without ideological training, and born into the systemic failure of Venezuela's social infrastructure—became a celebrated anti-hero among criminal circles.

In a nation where opportunity died long ago, the rise of figures like Niño Guerrero is not accidental. It is the inevitable outcome of a subsistence system where crime is rewarded, chaos is leveraged politically, and the state uses criminality as both a weapon and a shield.

In Venezuela, such figures gain status, notoriety, and mythological significance, even as they face near-certain death or incarceration. They are tools of political repression, currency in underground economies, and living proof that in a narco-state, violence is virtue.

Tren de Aragua's Militant Expansion Across Latin America

Between 2015 and 2016, Venezuela reached some of the highest crime and homicide rates in the world. Armed gangs launched coordinated attacks against Bolivarian police stations, checkpoints, and personnel. The Venezuelan Violence Observatory (OVV) recorded over 28,000 violent homicides in 2016 alone. Amid this chaos, Tren de Aragua fortified its position, engaging in direct armed conflict with state forces, killing over 20 police officers, and seizing control of urban territories.

Ironically, by 2018, homicide rates in Venezuela began to drop—not because of institutional success, but because the violence had shifted beyond its borders.

From Cúcuta in Colombia to Tulcán in Ecuador, and further into Tacna and Tarapacá in Peru and Chile, regional law enforcement began noticing a disturbing pattern: a new criminal order was establishing itself within migrant routes and border cities.

By 2019, Colombia's Attorney General had opened multiple investigations linked to Niño Guerrero's network. One such case centered on Norte de Santander, where Tren de Aragua operatives clashed with the Clan del Golfo—a powerful paramilitary successor group. These initial confrontations would only mark the beginning of a wider and bloodier campaign.

2020: Consolidation of a Criminal Insurgency

According to Colombian Ministry of Defense intelligence, the group—still directed from inside Tocorón Prison—began asserting itself not only in narcotics and extortion but also in armed confrontations with the ELN, FARC dissidents, and Residual Armed Groups (GAOR).

An ultra-classified 2020 report stated:
"The participation of this gang in activities such as homicides, extortion, and kidnappings has become evident in cities like Bogotá, Popayán, Cali, Pasto, Cúcuta, and Bucaramanga. Their modus operandi includes recording crimes and uploading them to social media to terrorize local populations and assert dominance over rival criminal entities, including GAORs."

In Cúcuta, the epicenter of their operations in Colombia, Tren de Aragua consolidated a financial stranglehold, dominating:

- Micro-trafficking networks
- Contraband and smuggling routes
- Human trafficking corridors, particularly exploiting Venezuelan migrants
- Extortion systems targeting sex workers, charging fees for territory control
- Coercive tolls for migrants crossing borders or bus terminals

This model was then replicated across the Andean corridor.

From Local Cells to Urban Occupation

The Colombian report further revealed how Tren de Aragua operates through "cars"—localized criminal units of roughly 30 members, each specializing in:
- Armed action
- Surveillance and intelligence
- Drug distribution
- Street-level extortion
- Organized robbery and control of prostitution zones

Each unit acts as a military cell within an expanding insurgent architecture, designed not merely to survive, but to displace and absorb local gangs or rivals.

Through intimidation, executions, and public messaging, they have absorbed smaller gangs, killed resisting actors, and filled the vacuum left by weakened state institutions—especially during the COVID-19 pandemic, when enforcement retreated and criminal economies flourished.

The Transnational Web: Tren de Aragua's Operational Control Across Borders

By 2021, when Peruvian authorities launched their first operations against Venezuelan criminal factions, the expansion of El Tren de Aragua across South America was no longer speculation—it was a confirmed reality. That same year, the Colombian Prosecutor's

Office, through extensive phone interceptions, uncovered the operational depth and financial structure of the group's human trafficking enterprise.

In Cúcuta, a border city that had become a major corridor for migrant flow, a Colombian national known as "Nino" was recorded receiving frequent wire transfers to coordinate migrant smuggling via long-distance buses. In one intercepted call, he said:

"They [Tren de Aragua] have people all along the border... in Bogotá, in Ipiales. They cross through the trails and go all the way up to Ecuador, Peru, Chile. It's all theirs. They report to one boss... They're probably making $5,000 to $6,000 a week."

This single statement unveiled a sophisticated transnational command structure—a criminal logistics network stretching from Colombia's Caribbean border to the Southern Cone, controlling routes, personnel, and territory like a shadow cartel-state.

Clashing Criminal Empires: Tren de Aragua vs. FARC Dissidents

By 2020, the group had already embedded itself in Nariño, Colombia, particularly in Pasto and Ipiales, the final cities before crossing into Ecuador. Intelligence reports confirmed that Tren de Aragua was competing for territorial dominance with the Second Marquetalia, a dissident FARC faction led by Iván Márquez, one of the last historical guerrilla leaders.

The Colombian Prosecutor's Office based its findings on the confession of Jackson Murillo López, alias Flaco, a local commander of Second Marquetalia in Ipiales. His testimony painted a disturbing picture: Venezuelan criminal groups were challenging historic Colombian insurgents, threatening their illicit economies and territorial control.

"I was ordered to clean the Aragua Train from the area," Flaco admitted.

His unit responded with extortion, the distribution of death threats, and armed resistance. The objective was clear: prevent the takeover of border towns and criminal economies—including the lucrative business of charging migrants, smugglers, and local sex workers for passage.

This confrontation marked a new hybrid war: not between state and insurgency, but between fragmented paramilitary remnants and transnational narco-terrorist franchises. In the words of Flaco:

"The landowners charge one or two dollars per migrant. It's big business... We charged them one million pesos a week [~$220] for protection from the Aragua Train, who robbed, extorted—even killed."

The Infiltration of Peru: Five Years of Criminal Embedding

As with Colombia and Ecuador, the penetration of Tren de Aragua into Peru occurred in parallel with the Venezuelan migration crisis, particularly after 2018. According to Peru's Ministry of Interior, over 1.34 million Venezuelans entered the country between 2018 and late 2023—81.6% via land routes, primarily from Ecuador.

The years 2018 and 2019 marked the peak of arrivals, with over 1.25 million people crossing into Peru in that period alone. While most were fleeing hunger and repression, Tren de Aragua used the humanitarian flow as cover to implant its operatives, cells, and logistical support networks.

One of the earliest signs of their presence occurred in August 2018, when Peru's Criminal Investigation Division (Divincri) arrested five Venezuelan nationals who were preparing an armed bank robbery at Plaza Norte Mall in Lima's Independencia district. The police referred to the group as "Los Malditos del Tren de Aragua"—an ominous branding that would soon become common in Peruvian headlines.

Criminal Architecture in Peru: From "Catire" to Factions of Terror

Among the earliest captured members of El Tren de Aragua in Peru was Edison Agustín Barrera, alias Catire—a Venezuelan national with a known history of contract killings. His arrest in August 2018 marked a pivotal moment in the operational expansion of the organization within the country.

Catire, whose nickname refers to light-haired individuals in Venezuelan slang, embodied the emerging prototype of the transnational criminal operative: young, brutal, unideological, but deeply embedded within the mafia ecosystem born from Venezuela's criminalized state.

In a leaked intelligence report from the Colombian Army dated January 2022, Catire was officially identified as the coordinator of Tren de Aragua's operations in Peru—a clear sign that the group's continental ambitions were being executed with strategic intent. A year after his initial arrest, in June 2019, the Eighth Preparatory Investigation Court of Lima Norte sentenced him to eight years in prison for illegal possession of weapons, ammunition, explosives, and for membership in a criminal organization.

But Catire was just the first wave. In the years that followed, Peruvian authorities identified multiple other leaders of the Aragua network, including:
- Freddy Xavier Romero Sulbarán, alias Machelo
- José Ángel Ortega Padrón, alias Armando
- Héctor Alfonso Prieto Materano, alias Mamut
- Yomar José Delgado Palacios, alias Nino

These individuals have been linked to a range of crimes: armed robbery, extortion, contract killings, kidnapping, homicide, arms trafficking, drug smuggling, organized crime, and human trafficking.

Human Trafficking: The Economic Engine of Expansion

According to General Carlos Malaver, director of Peru's Directorate Against Human Trafficking and Illicit Smuggling of Migrants (DIRCTPTIM), human trafficking is the backbone of the Aragua Train's criminal structure in the country. It is through this lucrative trade that the group consolidated its presence in Lima as well as key regional hubs such as La Libertad, Lambayeque, and Piura.

El Tren de Aragua does not operate as a singular cell but rather as a layered architecture of criminal factions. Peruvian police and prosecutors have identified five main factions under the organization's umbrella, each with internal leadership but ultimately reporting back to the central command in Venezuela. These are:

1. Los Gallegos
2. Hijos de Dios
3. Puros Hermanos Sicarios
4. Dinastía Alayón
5. Cota 905

The first two are considered the executive leadership within Peru—more numerous and more operationally expansive. According to Colonel Víctor Revoredo, head of the Homicide Division and Special Unit on Foreign Criminal Organizations, these factions represent the upper echelon of operational command.

Meanwhile, Puros Hermanos Sicarios, Dinastía Alayón, and Cota 905 are described as secondary in influence but remain active in several districts. Each faction is subdivided into smaller gangs, usually composed of three to five individuals, tasked with specific criminal functions—extortion, surveillance, armed enforcement, or control over prostitution rings.

Despite their decentralization, these units share one common trait:

"They all answer to El Niño Guerrero," states Revoredo.

An Invisible Network: Fragmented but Synchronized

Senior prosecutor Jorge Chávez Cotrina, national coordinator of the Specialized Prosecutor's Offices against Organized Crime, emphasizes that the group's compartmentalized structure is precisely what makes it resilient and hard to dismantle:

"Each line operates independently, with its own members. Members of one line don't know those in another. They're autonomous, yet all report to leaders abroad."

This cellular fragmentation—a structure reminiscent of terrorist networks—complicates investigative work. It also enables the organization to evade full exposure, even after major arrests.

A data analysis by OjoPúblico tracking arrests, operations, convictions, and preventive detentions between 2018 and October 2023 confirmed that at least 219 individuals affiliated with the Tren de Aragua were captured in Peru. The majority were connected to the factions Los Gallegos, Puros Hermanos Sicarios, and Dinastía Alayón.

> Within these factions, micro-gangs have emerged, including:
> - Los Gatilleros de San Martín de Porres
> - Los Chamos de la Hacienda de San Juan de Lurigancho
> - Los Trantes de Lince

Yet, not all who claim the name "Tren de Aragua" truly belong to it. General Malaver warns that many smaller gangs brandish the group's name as a form of criminal marketing:

"It's a seal. A brand. Saying you're part of the Aragua Train inspires fear. Some use the name just to extort or carry out crimes more easily."

The Tren de Aragua: A Criminal State Franchise Operating Across Borders

The expansion of the Tren de Aragua is not merely a Venezuelan export; it is a transnational criminal mutation forged from the collapse of state authority and institutional complicity. Originally formed within Venezuela's prison system and construction unions under Hugo Chávez's rule, this group consolidated its power under Nicolás Maduro and allies like Tareck El Aissami, evolving into a continental structure with operations across Colombia, Ecuador, Peru, and Chile.

Since 2018, amid the Venezuelan migration crisis, the Tren de Aragua has exploited state fragility in the Andean region to expand its operations, replacing local criminal groups and gaining control of key urban territories — known as "plazas" — particularly in Peru.

In Lima and across 14 districts of the capital, the group engages in extortion, contract killings, arms trafficking, drug distribution, and — most critically — human trafficking for sexual exploitation. Using debt bondage, psychological manipulation, and transnational mobility, the organization enslaves hundreds of women, primarily from Venezuela, Colombia, and Ecuador. These women are rotated between cities like Lima, Arequipa, and Cajamarca, ensuring maximum control and disorientation.

The Peruvian Police and Prosecutor's Offices have documented the existence of at least five internal factions — including Los Gallegos, Hijos de Dios, and Dinastía Alayón — each operating with a degree of autonomy, yet all responding to top-level leadership based in Venezuela. Arrests of high-ranking figures such as Edison "Catire" Barrera and Yomar "Nino" Delgado confirm the presence of a well-organized, decentralized criminal governance model that mimics military command structures.

Their activities yield millions in illicit profits annually. In just one 2022 report, the Los Gallegos faction was estimated to earn over 4.4 million soles per year from forced prostitution in Lima alone. The "plaza" system — strategically placed near nightclubs, hotels, and commercial centers — serves as a retail hub of sexual exploitation and extortion.

What makes this structure even more difficult to dismantle is its fluid and dynamic nature: criminals interchange roles regularly (gunmen become informants, collectors act as lookouts), and victims are kept in permanent transit. This rotational strategy thwarts identification and weakens institutional responses.

Yet the implications transcend local crime.

Transnational Threats and U.S. Exposure

The United States has become a secondary theatre of operation — not through direct violent action, but via illicit financial flows, infrastructure reconnaissance, and disinformation. Entities tied to Chavismo and its criminal-military-industrial complex engage in money laundering, manipulation of political narratives, and attempts to compromise democratic institutions.

Infiltration into critical sectors — from banking to energy — alongside intelligence activity near U.S. infrastructure, underscores a dangerous escalation: a convergence of narco-terrorism, populist authoritarianism, and criminal diplomacy. These networks do not merely smuggle drugs — they traffic influence, destabilize democracies, and position themselves as parallel power structures.

A Region at the Tipping Point

The Western Hemisphere now confronts an unprecedented convergence: terrorists, cartels, corrupt regimes, and failed states cooperating in a common front against institutional order. Their methods are not isolated — they are systemic, coordinated, and expanding.

Latin America stands at a threshold — either to reclaim its institutions, or to become a permanent laboratory of hybrid warfare, narco-politics, and state criminality.

As such, the response cannot be fragmented. It requires:
- Integrated regional cooperation,

- Recognition of Venezuela as a criminal state prototype,
- Judicial mechanisms that transcend borders,
- And the moral courage to speak truths where diplomacy has failed.

Closing Note

What we face is not just a cartel. It is a criminal paradigm, forged in the ruins of Bolivarianism and exported with impunity. The time has come to address it not merely as a law enforcement matter — but as a geopolitical emergency.

If we fail to name the enemy, we risk normalizing it. And if we normalize it, we have already lost.

Chapter 6
Conclusion

A Testament of Truth in Times of Complicity

Dear Reader,

If you have reached this point, you have not only read a book — you have borne witness to something far deeper. Dangerous Times is not just a geopolitical analysis. It is the documentary birth certificate of a new criminal era, one in which Venezuela — once a democratic republic — has now fully morphed into a narco-terrorist state, exporting instability, corruption, and violence across the globe.

This book represents one of the last—and perhaps most urgent—calls for clarity and action. It is part of a broader project that seeks to unmask an evolving prototype: a regime that weaponizes poverty, manipulates migration, destroys dissent, and uses organized crime as a tool of foreign policy. This model has found willing partners in cartels, extremist networks, and rogue governments. And as the world enters a period of volatile transformation—marked by wars, realignments, and systemic collapse—the Venezuelan regime has thrived in the shadows.

While the international community focuses on global crises, the regime in Caracas consolidates power, refines its criminal machinery, and extends its reach. The Cartel of the Suns, Tren de Aragua, and allied armed groups are no longer local actors. They have become global franchises—operating in the United States, Canada, Europe, and across Latin America. Whether openly acknowledged or not, the presence is real. The threat is active. And the silence surrounding it is strategic.

Let us be unequivocal:

Venezuela today is not just a failed state — it is an operational hub of global narco-terrorism.

It is a regime that launders billions, traffics people, destabilizes elections, and protects terrorists.

And it does so while wrapping itself in the rhetoric of sovereignty, diplomacy, and revolution.

This conclusion is not written in bitterness — it is written in resistance.

Because to document this reality is, in itself, an act of defiance.

Throughout this journey, I have received testimonies, walked through zones of criminal control, spoken with victims, investigators, and intelligence officers from across the hemisphere. The pattern is clear. What we face is not fragmented violence. It is a system. A criminal state system, with ideological camouflage and diplomatic immunity.

And while governments debate and NGOs tiptoe around the terminology, the regime continues to kill, imprison, torture, silence, traffic, and expand.

We are facing a hybrid threat without precedent:
- A government that behaves like a cartel.
- A cartel that speaks the language of diplomacy.
- A revolution that has become a transnational criminal empire.

The question now is not whether the threat exists — it is whether we will have the courage to confront it.

This book is the first in a series. Together with a multidisciplinary team of analysts, legal experts, journalists, survivors, and former operatives, we will continue to expose the web of alliances, the financial structures, and the operational mechanisms of narco-terrorist regimes.

But for now, I leave you with this truth:

What grows in the silence of institutions can one day bring down nations.
We must not remain observers.
We must not negotiate with terror.
We must not allow history to be rewritten by criminals in suits.

If the Tren de Aragua is the criminal ambassador of Maduro's regime, then this book is our counter-declaration of sovereignty, memory, and resistance.

Thank you for reading. Thank you for standing.
We are not alone.
But we must act — while there is still time.

— Johan Obdola

About the Author

A Life of Duty and Purpose

"I have lived a life forged in the crucible of conflict and conviction—not by design, but by necessity. Mine has been a journey where duty overruled comfort, and truth often demanded sacrifice. The passage of time has blurred many of the details, yet what remains vivid are the wounds: not only those on my body, but those carved deep into the soul by betrayal, loss, silence, and the weight of responsibility.

I have fallen, yes. But I have also risen, again and again. I have felt the sting of shame, the unbearable weight of knowing I could not save everyone who trusted me. And yet, I have known moments of pride—rare and luminous—where I was able to protect, to resist, to speak, and to fight when others stayed silent. These are the moments that remind me why I continue.

Hope has been my only luxury. In times of darkness, it has been the light that kept me breathing. When I walked alone through exile, through war zones, through rooms of power and corridors of fear, hope never abandoned me. Even now, it walks beside me.

If there is a message in my story, it is this: a single voice, no matter how silenced or battered, can still hold the line. Our future demands that we do not retreat into cynicism. Instead, we must awaken—to reclaim courage, to rebuild justice, to restore our sense of collective responsibility in a fractured world." Johan O.

About the Author: Johan Obdola

Johan Obdola is not merely a witness to history—he is one of its active defenders. Born in Venezuela and now a Canadian citizen, Johan has dedicated over three decades to the fight against narco-terrorism, state corruption, transnational crime, and the erosion of global security. A survivor of assassination attempts and political persecution, Johan was the first Venezuelan granted refugee status in Canada as a result of his war against organized crime.

A pioneering intelligence and geopolitical analyst, Johan's expertise has been forged in the most volatile regions on Earth. From the jungles of Latin America to the tribal territories of Asia and the Middle East, he has served as a consultant, negotiator, and strategist for national governments, military institutions, and global security coalitions. He has directly advised institutions such as NATO, the OAS, INTERPOL, and EUROPOL, and has collaborated with counter-narcotics agencies in Colombia, Trinidad and Tobago, Oman, the UAE, and beyond.

Johan is the founder and current president of IOSI Global (International Organization for Security and Intelligence), a multinational platform with over 80,000 members dedicated to confronting emerging security threats and building ethical frameworks for action. He is also the founder of PRAEON Advisory, a private geopolitical intelligence firm.

His work is not only institutional—it is deeply human. Johan has worked side-by-side with indigenous tribes in the Amazon and North America, defending their rights and advocating for justice in forgotten regions. He has built bridges between intelligence operations and cultural resilience, proving that security is not merely military, but civilizational.

He has been featured in leading international media, including Fox News, Infobae, Daily Star, and the Washington Examiner. A sought-after speaker on counterterrorism, governance collapse, and hybrid threats, Johan brings a rare synthesis of field experience, policy acumen, and moral clarity.

In 2024, he published his first book, *Dangerous Times: The Americas Under the Shadows of Terror*, exposing Venezuela's descent into a narco-terrorist state and its hemispheric consequences. This work is the first in a multi-volume series examining the global dimensions of transnational organized crime, institutional failure, and the urgent call for ethical leadership.

Johan Obdola's life and work remind us that in an age of disinformation and disorder, truth still matters—and those who stand for it, even in silence or exile, are never alone. He continues to offer his expertise to governments, institutions, and communities across the globe, advancing a singular mission: to defend what remains, and to help build what must come next.

DANGEROUS TIMES. Book Series

A Global Intelligence Chronicle by Johan Obdola & Collaborators

Editorial Note

DANGEROUS TIMES is not merely a book series—it is a transcontinental testimony of a collapsing world order. Each volume is a strategic window into a region gripped by chaos, criminal convergence, and institutional failure. This series evolves across continents, integrating the voices of intelligence professionals, military experts, academics, field agents, diplomats, and civil society leaders who have lived the reality of conflict.

Although titles and subtitles may be refined as global developments unfold, the mission remains: to expose the underlying architecture of modern threats—and to offer credible, collective responses.

The final volume will reunite all participating co-authors from the series for a shared chapter of solutions, drawing from their lived experience and regional expertise to present actionable strategies for restoring global security and governance.

Book One

DANGEROUS TIMES: The Americas Under the Shadows of Terror

The Rise of Narco-Terrorism and State Capture in the Western Hemisphere

(Completed and Published)

Book Two

DANGEROUS TIMES: The Black Book of the Bolivarian Revolution

Anatomy of a Criminal State – The Venezuelan Prototype and its Global Export

Book Three

DANGEROUS TIMES: Hemispheric Collapse

Shadow Networks and Strategic Infiltration Across the Americas

Book Four

DANGEROUS TIMES: AFRICA – Echoes of Terror

From Warlords to Wagner: The New Frontiers of Conflict and Exploitation

Book Five

DANGEROUS TIMES: EUROPE – A Continent in Crisis

Hybrid Threats, Extremism, and the Fragmentation of Democratic Order

Book Six

DANGEROUS TIMES: THE MIDDLE EAST – Sandstorms of Extremism

Religions, Regimes, and the Long War of Influence

Book Seven

DANGEROUS TIMES: ASIA – Shadows of Power

Authoritarianism, Surveillance States, and the Geopolitics of Fear

Book Eight

DANGEROUS TIMES: The Empire of Blood Money

Unmasking the Global Financial Ecosystem of Narco-Terrorism

Book Nine

DANGEROUS TIMES: The Final Transynthesis

Collective Intelligence, Regional Perspectives, and Strategic Solutions to Global Threats

A concluding volume featuring joint contributions from all regional authors and collaborators—bridging analysis with action.

Possible Additional Volumes (Pending Development):

DANGEROUS TIMES: Oceania and the Indo-Pacific

New Routes of Trafficking, Espionage, and Strategic Competition.

www.ingramcontent.com/pod-product-compliance
Lightning Source LLC
Chambersburg PA
CBHW031149020426
42333CB00013B/584